RANCH

RANCH

PORTRAIT OF A SURVIVING DREAM

Photographs by Dudley Witney

Text by Moira Johnston

Doubleday & Company, Inc.
Garden City, New York
1983

Library of Congress Cataloging in Publication Data

Witney, Dudley.
    Ranch.

    1. Ranches—West (U.S.)   2. Ranches—Northwest,
Canadian.   3. Ranch life—West (U.S.)   4. Ranch life—
Northwest, Canadian.   5. West (U.S.)—Social life and
customs.   6. Northwest, Canadian—Social life and
customs.   I. Johnston, Moira   II. Title.
F595.2.J63 1983   779′.9978   82-45018
ISBN 0-385-18916-8

Designed and produced for
Doubleday and Company, Inc. by
Key Porter Books
59 Front Street East
Toronto, Canada M5E 1B3

First Edition

Design by Ken Rodmell

Typesetting by Imprint Typesetting, Toronto
Printing and Binding by Mandarin Offset Marketing (HK) Ltd.

Printed in Hong Kong

Frontispiece / Approaching the summer range, Pitchfork
    Ranch, Wyoming

Opposite / Padlock Ranch, Montana

Page 6 / Front porch, the old ranchhouse, Siggins Ranch,
    Cody, Wyoming

Page 7 / Cowboy, Padlock Ranch

Page 8 / Saddling up, Evans Camp Ranch, Buford, Colorado

Pages 10 and 11 / Cattle drive, Pitchfork Ranch

To Don and Christie and to Roger, Stephen, Sarah and Luke

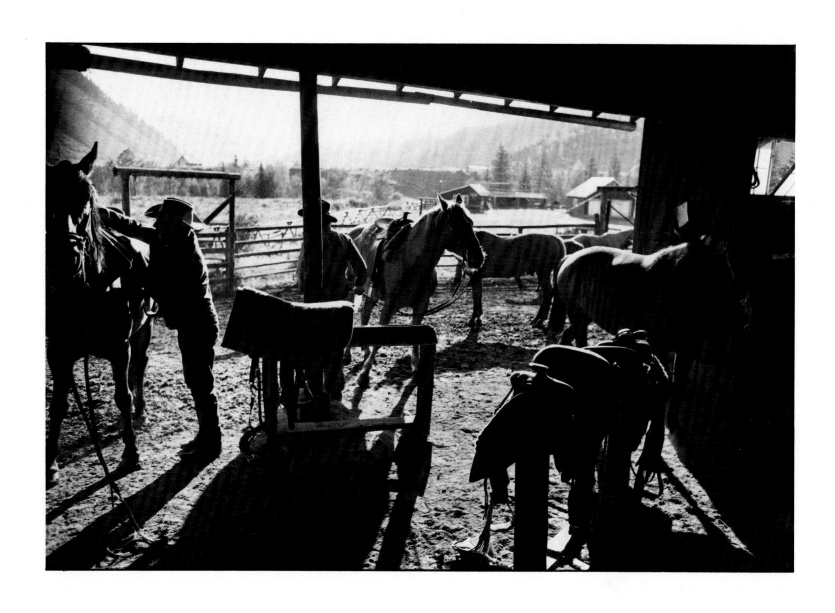

CONTENTS

THE JOURNEY

Grazing range near Stanley, New Mexico

Jack Cooper, veteran cowboy, Padlock Ranch, Montana

THE JOURNEY

IT'S DROUGHT!" Gordon Parke called over his shoulder as we saddled up for the cattle drive that would push 300 head of cattle up to the better grass at 7,000 feet. A hot, dry summer was scorching the Cariboo, the wild, mountain-locked plateau of gold-rich rivers, lakes and forest that is British Columbia's heartland. To me, it had always been magic to follow the Fraser River up from the sodden Pacific coast, emerge from the chasms and deep shadow of the Fraser Canyon, and see the Cariboo open into eroded folds of rangeland scattered with sage and golden sunflowers. For more than a quarter of a century, I had visited the Bonaparte Ranch, the oldest ranch in British Columbia still owned by the founding family, and watched Gordon ranch his remote Shangri-la in Upper Hat Creek Valley. This year, his range was a tinderbox, the grasses parched and stunted. Hat Creek, essential to the greening of the valley's hayfields, had shrunk to a weak trickle. The valley floor was still green with the irrigated fields of oat and alfalfa that would supply the vital winter hay, but the creek was too low to water thirsty cattle.

We were to push the cattle up to the summit of the range that rose from the valley floor. It was not a time when Gordon needed amateurs, but he had permitted me to come. We gathered the cattle from bald, brown hills, then encircled them in a deep gully, holding them while Gordon, his cowboy and the better riders collected the stragglers. Two big bulls pawed the ground and heaved their heavy necks back and forth rhythmically, eyes blazing. Restive, the cows pressed out against our small ring of riders, and I welcomed the horses' intuitive wheeling to cut them off. Keeping an anxious eye on the bulls, I looked up in disbelief at the steep, pine-covered face ahead of us. Like a general planning a military assault, Gordon ordered: "Once we get them moving, we've got to keep them moving." He slapped his thigh and yelled, "Hy-yah!" And it began. Choking dust flew up from rusty pine needles and loose rocks as our horses plunged straight up the mountainside, scrambling for footholds. My saddle slipped back, exposing wet, foaming hide. I clutched the horn and pitched forward on my horse's neck, terrified that I would slide off under the hooves of the cattle and bulls bawling all around me in the frenzied charge through the pine forest. Pine snags tore at us like barbed wire; one ripped across my leg, raising a long welt under the denim. My horse reared back, cracking the ridge of his neck against my eye, stunning me. But all that mattered in those wild moments was hanging on and keeping the momentum going uphill. "Hy-yah! Hy-yah! *Move* it! *Move* it! Get up there!"

And then, with a sense of deliverance, we had burst out into open sky and a sea of deep shrubs and range grass, the cattle galloping in with ravenous abandon, trampling spikes of red Indian paintbrush and blue lupin underfoot as they swam, knee-high, through the grass. A snow-flecked glacial bowl fanned out above us. I could see fragments of the green valley beyond the forested humps we had just conquered. The sense of liberation and beauty was overwhelming. I had done something I had never believed I could do. As I exulted, the Girl of the Golden West, Gordon galloped down a precipitous grass hillside to break up the two bulls who'd plunged, battling, down the slope. The two bellowing herd sires were struggling for mastery, horns locked. With horrified fascination, we watched Gordon's horse rear in the midst of the fight as he tried to prod the bulls apart. He pushed them back to the herd and galloped back up to us, amused at my awe, and set out a pink salt lick at the summit, like a cairn. The cows stampeded for it. "It'll hold these beggars for awhile, but they'll drift down again, trying to get back to the home ranch. We'll have to push them back up every day or so."

For me, the drive had been a lifetime event, a day of intense contrasts: of risk and joy, sweat and splendor, of singular terror and friendly banter. For Gordon, it had been just another ranching day, one he would repeat again and again throughout the summer.

Pushing into the Pacific thirty miles north of Santa Barbara Point Conception is a spit of land where north and south Califor-

Prehistoric petroglyph. Ladder Ranch, New Mexico.

nia abut. It is a place of opposites. Warm and cold ocean currents clash, and tides meet in combat, strewing ships along the beach. Even the range—the grasses and shrubs, and the winds and rains that shape them—is split; what thrives on one side shrivels on the other. But one great fact overrides the conflicts: the winter rains and moist Pacific fogs lay down a carpet of grass deeper and greener than any Gordon Parke ever sees, making this small peninsula one of the crown jewels of American ranchlands. "This is cow heaven," Brad Lundborg laughs, pointing toward a group of cattle luxuriating in the shade of an oak like pampered harem queens as we rattled by pickup over the hills of the El Cojo-Jalama Ranch Brad manages, a 24,000-acre spread running 2,000 head. This is grass that can fatten a cow on only ten acres—superrange, by the measure of some New Mexican ranchers hard-pressed to fatten a cow on 100. As rich in history as it is in grass, the ranch is the scene each spring of the traditional "run through the mustard," when Brad and his cowboys round up cattle lost in hills that become an enveloping sea of yellow-blooming mustard as high as a horse's head. One of the great mythic images of California's rancho era, it ties Brad to the days when Mexican and Spanish land grant ranchos sprawled north along the California coast from San Diego to Redding like feudal baronies. For the coastal grass and the unsurpassed beauty of the land—oak-strewn mesas and hills rolling back from a ravishing coastline—lured rancheros, their cattle and horses, and allowed the cattle culture that trailed up from Mexico into North America with the padres and conquistadors to reach perhaps its fullest expression. Here, cattle and their hides became the stuff of life, the measure of wealth, the source of status and lifestyle. As close to extinction now as the condor, the few ranches clustered at Point Conception are among the last of California's great rancho lands surviving with grasslands intact, still running cattle.

Brad doesn't own the land and he has no Spanish blood. But he has spent his life within a day's ride of El Cojo-Jalama, always working on, or within sight of, the ranches of Point Conception. And he takes a fierce pride in keeping the cattle operation working against odds, and the traditions of America's first cowboy, the vaquero, alive. He ducks under long strips of rawhide that are stretched to dry between trees in his backyard as he heads for the tack room to saddle up. In the winter, he braids the rawhide into reatas, or lassos, in the vaquero way. Using engraving tools he has fashioned out of hayrake teeth, he has made his

19

Buckaroo-style bit.

spurs and the circular silver conches that decorate the bridle. With deliberate ceremony, he cinches on a modified version of the traditional Visalia saddle, its leather embellished with floral carving and silver—"but not a lot of silver," Brad stresses. He wears the knee-length chaps, or chinks, that evolved in the thorny scrub ranges of Mexico and southern California, and uses the long stirrup flaps, the tapaderos, that gave flamboyance to the vaquero's style. But, as with the trappings of the ancient Scythian horseman, the beauty of the style lies in embellishing the functional. "It protects you from getting squishy wet from the dew. It doesn't matter how good you look if you can't get the work done," he says, as he puts his Appaloosa mare through the exquisite moves handed down for 190 years to Brad. For he is part of the rich tapestry of cowboys and farmers woven into the history of these hills.

But like the tides and winds that have always converged on the point, social forces are gathering to a crescendo. In spite of Brad's lean management style, the El Cojo-Jalama is only marginally profitable in a volatile beef market, able to continue as a cattle ranch because its owner, the Bixby Ranch Company, has a buffer of revenues from oil and land holdings in Long Beach. Next to the ranch, the Vandenberg Air Force Base, which has already gobbled the Suden Ranch, flexes its muscles, looking to expand its missile base. Point Conception has been targeted by the state's utilities commission as the site of a massive liquified natural gas terminal, a highly controversial project that, like the oil rigs drilling just offshore, could profoundly alter the landscape and lifestyle of the region in the name of the greater good. The Coastal Commission responds to the growing public clamor for access to pristine beaches by putting pressure on El Cojo-Jalama and its neighbor, the famous Hollister Ranch, to allow public roads through their ranches. Brad's full-time guard is busier than ever patrolling the ranch for trespassers who start fires and leave fences open, and for rustlers whose numbers grow with the price of beef and the swift convenience of pickups, radios and helicopters. In five minutes, rustlers can shoot a cow, saw through the animal with a power saw and be off in a pickup truck.

The ranches at Point Conception lie within reach of Los Angeles, whose insatiable appetite for land devours open space from Orange County to Santa Barbara. The region's seductive ranches are being courted by developers. Ronald Reagan's small recreational ranch in nearby Santa Ynez Valley attracts increasing numbers of wealthy hobby ranchers and horsebreeders, and

Working chaps worn by a Paducah, Texas, cowboy.

raises land prices beyond the realm of practical agriculture. There is currently a tax incentive for keeping the land agricultural, but it is not carved in stone, nor is it a panacea for ranching's marginal economics. The Hollister Ranch has already fallen, split up and sold off in 100-acre lots, its century-old cattle operation trying to coexist with weekending Los Angelenos. Historically, development has been the kiss of death to working ranches. San Julian's Dibblee Poett, most deeply rooted of any of the local ranchers, has so far resisted offers to sell, but now runs only a token herd on range that has shrunk over the years to just a tenth of the domain his ancestors controlled.

The western ranch is the home and heart of a uniquely North American culture that has become the world's dream. Its basic function is to harvest grass and convert it to protein. But for more than four centuries, it has also fed the soul and stirred and satisfied primordial longings. It has created the cowboy and spawned as much mythology as Mount Olympus. For the millions of us who have drifted from the land, it survives as a spiritual home, a storehouse of values we can call on if needed, like winter hay. Now, ranches stand as the best and possibly last line of defense for land that, over centuries—through thousands of subtle and cataclysmic adaptations—evolved to a natural climax state of grass, the grass that had covered nearly half the continent when Europeans first arrived.

Though not raised on a ranch, I am a child of the west, roped from birth to affectionate images of ranching. I was raised on my father's stories of his years on an Argentinian *estancia*, riding with the gauchos who had grown from the same Spanish source as the vaqueros of California. I used to run my fingers through the silky, mountain-goat chaps my father had worn as a young Mountie when he patrolled the range and forests of the Cariboo, a region whose gold rush had, like California's, spurred a struggling young cattle industry on to lusty growth. An earlier generation of young Mounties—gentlemen horsemen seeking adventure—had come to the western provinces to keep the early settlers in order, and hundreds had left the Force to become Canada's pioneer ranchers.

I had more recently become familiar with some of the California ranches and now was eager to go beyond my west coast experience and look at ranches from a broader perspective. Sometimes travelling alone, sometimes accompanied by my young daughter, I drove the cattle road from El Paso to the

Early adobe ranchhouse in Pecos, New Mexico. In the southwest, local clay mixed with straw, shaped and dried in molds, then baked in the sun, created adobe bricks, an inexpensive and attractive building material that offered good insulation. But, easily decayed by weather, they required loving care and repair.

Cariboo, from Cheyenne to Santa Barbara, hoping to gain some sense of the true state of the ranch. I wanted to find it strong.

Although Point Conception was already as green as English countryside, it was winter when I started out, when the bones of ranches in most states and Canada would be bared. In the cycle of the year, it was the moment of calm before calving, branding, haying and driving cattle from winter to summer range, when there was time to visit.

As I drove to El Paso in the western tip of Texas where New Mexico, Texas and Mexico converge, I tried to imagine the country with no boundaries. It was all Spanish when the first cattle straggled across the Rio Grande, the river that runs south from its source in Colorado and then turns eastward to become the boundary between Mexico and Texas before spilling into the Gulf of Mexico. The cattle saga had begun in the grasslands of south central Mexico, east of Guadalajara, several hundred miles to the south. Just thirty years after the *Mayflower* arrived, skinny, long-horned cattle had bawled in the holds of Spanish ships heading for Mexico, brought by Cortés to feed and clothe his soldiers. These would form the nucleus of herds for the missions in California and the southwest that would claim lands and souls for Christ as well as for Spain, and for the great ranchos that would build up around them. The cattle propagated and fanned out, following grass and water, trailing north with the priests and conquistadors like camp followers, turned out, at times, to go wild on the range.

I had never seen the Rio Grande. And I prepared for it by envisioning the river free of the boundary and water politics that now cloud it, a resting and watering spot for heroic cattle drives,

Cemetery at Galisteo is a reminder that the Spanish thrust northward died in New Mexico, overwhelmed by the westward-moving cattle frontier.

often many hundred miles long, before railways and trucks. I conjured up El Paso as a lively cowtown with vaqueros, not Yankee cowboys, in dashing riding gear that fused the grandeur that had been Spain with the reality of the frontier: wrapped sashes, silver trappings, the flapping tapaderos Brad Lundborg had worn over his stirrups, and an élan and skill on horseback that has never been surpassed, even by the Indians.

The Rio Grande and the El Paso it flows through today do not support romantic fantasy. A monument to the U.S. Army Corps of Engineers, the river is a concrete trough encasing a finger-deep film of water over mud, a pathetic trickle sucked dry for the chili and cotton fields upriver before it reaches El Paso. And El Paso! An overgrown cowtown, a treeless sprawl of small houses, mobile homes and oil drilling equipment leap-frogging over forbidding hills. Even in winter, the town looked parched and thirsty, and I could understand the passion for water that was fuelling the fight to drill New Mexico's ground water and pipe it south to support El Paso's growth, a battle intensified by lingering Civil War biases, for New Mexico had been Union and Texas Confederate, a schism of spirit and politics that persists.

There had been no one historic cattle trail north, but the

23

earliest had led north into New Mexico. The first was Coronado's expedition in 1540, which had trailed the very first cattle up through Arizona into New Mexico, and Juan de Onate's drive north along the Rio Grande almost to Taos in 1598. The sheep, goats, horses and 7,000 head of cattle that had joined Onate's remarkable journey became the source of survival for the Spanish settlements that took root here nearly 400 years before I set my car north on the superhighway that more or less traces the old trail. I tried to slow my mental pace and look with Onate's eyes for watering and stopping places every twelve or fifteen miles, the limit of a day's cattle drive.

A tumbleweed rolled across the road and perched on a fencepost, like a miniature tree, a sign of dry and wasting range. West of Las Cruces, towards Lordsburg, the grass looked immutably sparse. A sign warned of rattlesnakes. Cactus and creosote bush encroached on the ghost town of Shakespeare, whose entrance was fenced off and padlocked. "The soil's so thin and rocky, they used to have a saying in Shakespeare that if you shot somebody you had to dig his grave. You'd think twice about it. It sure kept down the shootin'," said Rita Hill, who, with her daughter Janaloo, ranches out of the former town. "Shakespeare, population two, and we're *it*!" she said, surveying the few crumbling adobe buildings that are all that remain of what had been a mining town of 2,000. Rita and her late husband, Frank, bought the ranch that contains Shakespeare and its precious springs in 1935, a year of drought and depression, "and we've been starving comfortably ever since."

Rita has the wise and weathered face of a veteran of half a century of struggling to ranch out of the adobe ruins of a lawless little silver mining town and to hold on to the land. Since the death of the husband she affectionately describes as "one of the last of the open-range cowboys," she and Janaloo have run it alone. Janaloo has the genteel, pale-powdered face and elegant carriage of a ballet dancer. "I wanted to be a dancer—until I grew the last three inches. And I had acting ambitions . . . ." Rita chirps in, "She danced before becoming a ranchhand. Danced in movies some. The Pasadena Playhouse. And she modelled in New York. I bet she's the only model in New York who could throw a diamond hitch!" "But the ranch needed somebody to take care of it," says Janaloo, "so I came home finally, and stayed."

To help supplement the income from cattle and preserve what remains of the town, the two women have attempted a

In the New Mexican ghost town of Shakespeare, rancher Janaloo Hill sits on the steps of the Grant House, the eating house and saloon that became the scene of hangings in the lawless mining town. Horse thieves and outlaws were hanged from the building's large brace timbers inside.

little alchemy, trying to turn the crumbling adobe into gold by a mild exploitation of its tourist potential. Now, on certain Sundays, Rita and Janaloo put on old-fashioned dresses and give tours of Shakespeare, telling the bloody stories of a boom town created out of desert by silver mines and a diamond swindle, of the spring that made it a lusty oasis on the gold rush and immigrant trail to California, a hideout for outlaws and the famous Texas cowboys who rustled Mexican cattle and drove them north to sell to the string of forts in the area. They live, without electricity, in what used to be the general store, and have turned an old barn into a dance studio for the little girls of nearby Lordsburg.

As I left to follow Onate's trail north, the two ladies lit the kerosene lamp for their evening's reading, and a pale light—so much paler than the remarkable spirit that kept it lit—brought a flicker of life to Shakespeare.

The Rio Grande looked more like the river the Spaniards would have seen as I followed it north to Taos. Cattle grazed in stubble fields and pecan orchards along the river, an interface of ranch-

25

ing and farming that faded out farther north as the Rio Grande became eroded gorges, purple shadow and poor range. At this point in his great cattle drive of 1598, Juan de Onate would still have had high hopes. For, more than colonizing ventures, his and others' had been a search for the legendary golden cities—the Seven Cities of Cibola, Quivira,—that, as gold from central and South American sources faded, had lured Spanish explorers into arid deserts and, ultimately, terrible disappointment. The pueblo at Taos, when it was eventually found in 1615, was of humble adobe, not gold.

Taos, a gentle eruption of adobe at the base of the snowy Sangre de Cristos, a southern spur of the Rockies, was remote enough that the Pueblo Indians and the Spanish who settled there have been able, even today, to retain some integrity of blood and culture, and to continue the pastoral way of life begun by Coronado's trickle of livestock. Here, in the region around Taos and Santa Fe, I moved into a poignant time warp, for the withering of the Spanish dream of a northern empire merges with the containment of the ancient Pueblo Indian culture. The Pueblo Indians' tribal herd of rangy, motley colored cattle grazing the wedge of rangeland west of the Taos Pueblo, do not have the straight-backed, beefy conformation required by mainstream ranchers.

The twisting drive along the Pecos River on a back road just east of Pecos was strewn along its length with adobe sheds and houses, some crumbling, some swelling into small villages or backyard ranches. Here were homemade, hand-to-mouth ranches, with chickens running under the feet of raw-boned cattle, burros and goats. In the middle of the road a cow and a calf, already several months old, spoke of the random breeding on the range that had been the Spanish way. Cattle towns of tin-roofed adobe churches and tiny roadside chapels, San Miguel and Villanueva belonged to a different world than Cheyenne or Miles City. The red-ochre of the local clay pervaded, spattering the silvered bases of sheds and lean-tos made of pinon sticks and rough-cut boards, and merging with the rusted corrugated roofs and iron rims of old wagon wheels. From the crumbling extrusions of shale to the slumped remains of adobe barns, the landscape was in an endless cycle of transition from rock to earth to brick and back to earth again.

The withdrawal of the Spanish presence became very real as I stood in the ruts of the Santa Fe Trail near Fort Union, north of Pecos, where the depressions of the old trail showed clearly in

Restaurant in Lordsburg, New Mexico.

the snow. They trace a path across a prairie of treeless meadow to the adobe ruins of the fort. It is powerful stuff, standing in the ruts of history, with the sounds and smells of Conestoga wagons, groaning wheels, great trains of oxen, cattle, soldiers, trappers, traders and settlers still carried in the wind.

Fort Union was a poignant place. For where the Spanish frontier had moved north behind a lasso, the American frontier moved west behind a plow. Metal cut rope. And even where cattle had come first, they were displaced wherever land would grow a crop. With the westward movement of the farming frontier, the early Spanish trails had been overlaid and criss-crossed with movement of Yankee cattle north and south, east and west, as they joined immigrant migrations and flowed toward newly established markets wherever they appeared. Contact of the two would mix the half-wild and casually bred Mexican-Spanish cattle with better breeds imported to the New World from Europe, and create the Texas longhorn, successor to the buffalo as it was exterminated from the plains. Gradually, the beefy Hereford, Angus and other British breeds would swell their numbers in the more northerly plains, and make their bid

27

"I'd faced everything—death, drought, hardship—but my good fortune put me in the hospital," says Floyce Masterson Bates of the shock of adjustment to the daily thousands of dollars that poured in from the first gas well she found after her husband's death forced her to run their west Texas ranch alone. A southern belle who came to this water-starved mesquite and rattlesnake-plagued range with a lacy, hand-made trousseau, she learned strength from the isolated setting and unyielding land. "Our oil and gas can be gone tomorrow," she says, "but the land will still be h   "

to replace the longhorn, a struggle for dominance that would be joined more recently by even beefier "exotic" breeds from Europe. Cattle power had passed to Texas, leaving the ranchero with little but his pride.

Oil wells announced Texas 100 miles before the border, like billboards. I was skirting the southern periphery of the Panhandle, the region that evokes images of drought and desperation, but yet also produced many of Texas' legendary ranches on its once-rich grasslands. Charlie Goodnight's, which once had 1,500 miles of barbed-wire fences and 150,000 cattle. The XIT and the Frying Pan. Heading toward Lubbock and Forth Worth, I moved through the west central plain of Texas, land that looks unfriendly. Mesquite, the dark-branched brambly shrub that spreads in dense forests here, was clearly the enemy. Ragged piles of mesquite stumps bulldozed out in an effort to reclaim the grass told the story. But there was also a dusting of palest green under the cap of dead-white grass, the new green spring grass just beginning to push up. I could sense the beauty that would be there in a month or two, and yet I would find a fierce regional attachment here that could not be fully explained by beauty, for the land simply does not have the splendor of parts of Montana, Wyoming or British Columbia. The people I met seemed to be living their lives, by passionate choice, within the radius of a handful of counties between Vernon and Abilene, moving from ranch to ranch as their parents had, creating a network of commitment to the Wagoner, the 6666, the Pitchfork, F Cross and Lambshead.

Fences were becoming to me a way of "reading" ranch country, a measure of prosperity and pride, and a guide to the local trees and building materials. A weathered old snake fence in the Cariboo—a silvery rickrack of fence running over miles of range like the Great Wall of China—is an incomparable sight. But at the town of Guthrie there was something fine about the spanking brick-red paint of the 6666's metal gates, corrals and corrugated steel sheds and barns. Slick, immaculate, efficient, they lacked warmth, but if ranches have personalities, the 6666 looked comfortable, confident and sophisticated. Its special glamor came from the fact that it is as rich in history as it is in oil and gas. It is the site of the largest gas well in the United States, and one of the few pioneer ranches still held by the founding family. The ranch is the legacy of Missourian Burk Burnett, who was bossing trail drives to the railhead at Abilene, Kansas, at 19,

Rancher Watt Matthews and his sisters, whose long lives on the historic Lambshead Ranch near Albany, Texas, are a living link with pioneer ranching in west Texas.

burning the 6666 brand into his own cattle at 21, and through the 1870s building a grassland empire that would extend from Texas into Oklahoma and New Mexico. Even today, the Burnett 6666 Ranches, headquartered at the 6666 contain an estimated 500,000 acres, making its heiress, Anne Phillips Sewel, the largest single property owner in Texas. Known affectionately as "Little Anne," to differentiate her from her late mother, "Miss Anne," she lives in Dallas and flies in by private jet to the ranch, where she has just redecorated the main house. Its interior was the most splendid of any I saw, an *Architectural Digest* dream of what a ranch house should be. A picture of the living room as it was hangs in the upstairs hall. The stuffed Texas longhorn heads that had flanked the stone fireplace have been replaced by massive elephant tusks, shot by Little Anne on African safari, and cowhides have been replaced by custom-woven carpets with southwest Indian motifs. The cowboys, as well as the family, eat in the formal dining room on a baronial slab of six-inch-thick polished wood under a chandelier of clustered antlers, ranch talk muffled by fabric wall coverings custom-printed with the 6666 brand. Yet, for all its lavishness, the 6666 is a serious working ranch.

Good working ranches come in many guises. As visibly historic as the 6666 is fashionable, the Lambshead, an hour's drive east of the 6666, has been preserved by the fabled Watt Matthews with a zeal that makes it a priceless example of Texas ranching history. In the Lambshead cookhouse, tradition reigns. Bottles of ketchup, honey and Kraft dressing, salt, pepper and pickles are the centerpiece on long, plain tables. Tin cups full of coffee that tastes like boiled iron and sweatbands, thick, salty chunks of bacon sliced from the wild hogs that live on the range, chili-laced cornbread and eggs fried on the blackened surface of a veteran stove are served up by an affable cook who, in the tradition of ranch cooks, controls his kitchen absolutely and makes his coffeepot part of a cowboy's toughening process. The Lambshead cookhouse, stacked with cattlemen's journals, its walls hung with collections of barbed wire, dusty bridles and cowboy hats, with its breakfast smells and bright light in the 5 a.m. blackness, was as inviting a sight as I had ever seen.

Another neighbor of the 6666, the century-old Pitchfork, had the sign "Hospitality Room for Ladies" hung above the bunkhouse door, a small herd of pickups outside the cookhouse at lunch time, and a row of cowboy hats hung in a row on a rail beside the door. I walked in to tomblike silence, with six cowboys sitting still at the long table, piles of chicken-fried steaks and potatoes, beans and gravy, pies and iced tea untouched before them. The cook's husband went out to the porch and pulled the rope on the big, old bell, the signal for the cowboys to attack the platters with a silent fury. In ten minutes it was over.

Then the afternoon's work began. Some heifers had got mixed in with the steers about ten miles back, and would have to be cut out and brought back by trailer to another pasture. At the barn, the six cowboys tied on their chaps and saddled their horses with working gear, then led their horses into a trailer, piled into two pickup trucks, pulling a small trailer for the heifers, and the entourage trailed out to the range, a ride that would have taken several hours on horseback. As they unloaded and trotted off, six abreast, wearing the black wide-brims that are cowboys' working hats, tan colored quilted parkas and leather chaps, I felt an overwhelming appreciation that, in spite of trucks, trailers and helicopters, this timeless sight was still possible—that there were still jobs pickups couldn't do.

It was an ancient play, and they all knew their parts. The cowboys moved into the mesquite, galloping onto the gentle, rolling range, disappearing and appearing again, as they fanned

Brangus cattle of the Ladder Ranch in New Mexico are deterred from escape by cattle guard and cowhides thrown over the gates.

out and ringed the cows, so smooth on their horses that when I could see only their heads and shoulders over the mesquite, they looked as if they were rolling on wheels. All slack and easy, slumped and loose-muscled, as they spaced themselves around the grazing brown and white Herefords, they slowly closed the ring, looking for the heifers they had to cut out. When a cowboy spotted one, his horse would explode into a wheeling gallop, until he was running flank to flank with the heifer. Swinging his rope into a swelling circle, he let it sail and settle around the heifer's neck. Whipping the rope tight around his horn—the act that has torn fingers off many a cowboy—he'd be off his horse and tying the calf by three feet in one fluid act, then tethering it to a mesquite until time to load it into the trailer. The classic pageant ended, as the six ambled back, all abreast, the job done in twenty minutes.

"These are good Texas cowboys," their cowboss, Billy George Drennan, said, "way better than average. They never say no, no matter what the job is. They can do everything. Not like the buckaroos that drift in here from time to time. They've got the chinks and the fancy saddles and all the style. But they won't get off their horses to fix a fence or feed the cows. They don't last a week."

Buckaroo, I was learning, has become a buzzword of the range. Basically, it is just another name for cowboy, the word used in Nevada and Oregon, where there are still huge spreads that maintain true horse-riding, cattle-punching cowboys. There, on remote ranges, buckaroos have been able to preserve the traditions, gear and dress of the old open-range cowboy. Like Brad Lundborg, they've kept alive some of the vaquero style that moved up the west coast from California. But the old buckaroo, I learned, has become a fad. Written up in *Western Horseman*

31

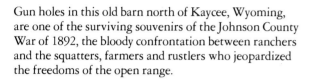

Gun holes in this old barn north of Kaycee, Wyoming, are one of the surviving souvenirs of the Johnson County War of 1892, the bloody confrontation between ranchers and the squatters, farmers and rustlers who jeopardized the freedoms of the open range.

magazine, mass-produced by saddle factories and western outfitters, glorified at rodeos, the "Buckaroo look" is being affected by everyone, everywhere. Featuring short chink chaps and extravagant Visalia saddles, "wild cloth" at the neck, jeans tucked into high boots, and big brim hats, the look is a mixture of the vaquero and the American cowboy of 100 years ago. For the true cowboy, adopting the buckaroo style is clearly part nostalgic pride. But it may also be an attempt to redefine himself at a time when the role of the mounted cowboy has been transformed and reduced by mechanization, and he has been forced to become an all-purpose ranchhand who can drive a tractor and fix the fences that have shrunk his freedoms, as well as ride a horse. In order to survive, most have had to adapt. But some, unable or unwilling to change, have drifted off to become itinerant buckaroos, locked to their saddles, tilting at change like Don Quixote. I hoped I would find an authentic buckaroo in his habitat.

At the Fort Worth Fat Stock Show, Lambshead's Watt Matthews sat in the auction arena, a semicircle of steeply pitched rows of seats around a small cattle ring and auctioneer's dais. At almost 84, Watt's face was smooth and youthful, his eyes and mind both snapping bright. "Uncle Watt" was surrounded by about a dozen of his family, who had flown in from Galveston, Colorado and Houston for his eighty-fourth birthday party that night, as he waited with a certain air of tension for his cattle to be sold. He enjoyed the status of owning one of west Texas' most historic ranches; he'd been awarded the Golden Spur as Rangeman of the

Old iron into decorative art.

Year, one of the proudest honors a rancher could earn; his mother was in the Cowboy Hall of Fame in Oklahoma City; he was surrounded by four generations of grandnieces, nephews and sisters. But he was a competitive rancher, not an historic monument. And when his cattle came up for sale, far more than income would be at stake. They were the reputation of his ranch in the eyes of other cattlemen, the measure of a lifetime's work.

Two-year-old Hereford bulls were sold first. With a staccato spiel, the auctioneer was bidding the bulls up to $3,000, $4,000, $6,000, lecturing the crowd good naturedly on how underpriced they were, while the handlers kept the bulls' noses up, prodded their feet into show position with their sticks and raked scrotums in the matter-of-fact way that strips any possible titillation from a rancher's preoccupation with the sexuality of his bulls. Cows are "a factory for producing calves." Bulls are for breeding. Both must produce "growthy" calves. If either fails to perform, or carries any defects, they are ruthlessly culled. As if he were telling me how to water my African daisies, a rancher whispered to me, "You want a dark scrotum, because sun can hurt the fertility of a pink one, and a dark one will produce cows with dark bags and teats that won't sunburn." The auctioneer was selling hard: "Four, four, four thousand. Do I hear $4,500. Here's your herd sire, fertility tested, ready to go to work. Forty-five hundred. Do I hear $5,000?"

Twenty of Watt Matthew's calves tumbled into the ring, charming the crowd, and overcoming the cool detachment of the ranchers' talk. They were followed by the cows, first-time mothers. "Here's your ticket, already on the ground," the auctioneer hustled, for calves are proof the cows can produce, and mother-up, a calf. They went for $925 a head. Watt allowed a slight twinkle, but kept busily making notes on other prices as lot after lot was sold. "Prices were good," he said at the end. "We got the third-highest prices." He'd enjoy his own birthday party.

Taking up what the Spanish had begun, Texas had sent cattle northward by the millions, following the Chisholm Trail through Oklahoma to the railheads at Abilene and Dodge City. The railroads had opened new eastern markets for Texas beef, markets badly needed after the devastation of the south in the Civil War. Where cattle and railroads came together, towns became rich and boisterous cattle bazaars, and the Midwestern states that had already plowed most of their natural grasslands evolved into the centers of cattle shipping and trading, of breeding and of finishing on grain and pasturing that they are today. The biggest stockyards are at Oklahoma City.

From Texas I followed parallel trails that had sent cattle streaming north into Wyoming and Montana to fill the grasslands vacated by the buffalo in the 1870s and '80s. Although only a brief drive from Taos, the cattle country round Cimarron in northern New Mexico was part of this mainstream, cut off from the Pueblo culture by the Sangre de Cristo Mountains, and, in terrain and climate, more akin to Colorado, just to the north. Crisscrossed too by the Santa Fe Trail, one of the major routes for settlers and cattle moving west from Missouri and Arkansas, it had felt the impact of the American tide. Dropping off Highway 25 that runs the length of the state, I drove down a long, ice-rutted county road and stopped at the sign CS Ranch. Almost out of sight of the road, I could see an appealing cluster of white ranch buildings set in a stand of mature trees. Sparkling hoarfrost coated barbed wire and turned branches into crisp white lace. Cattle, kept close to the home ranch for winter feeding, nosed the grass that bristled through the snow. With a backdrop of snowy mountains, a source of water and summer range, the scene had a comfortable, well-aged self-sufficiency, a deeply satisfying aesthetic that went beyond function. Ranches that have this quality are rare, but they are not period pieces. They pulse with life and a sense of practical purpose. But there is an ingredient more vital than water or a principality of grassland, I would learn. To be great, a ranch must have people who can match it.

The Davises had no warning that I was coming. The sun was low, snow deep from the previous night's storm, their county road almost impassable. My daughter and I were feeling lonely and vulnerable in this sparsely populated range country. I followed the smoke rising from one of several frame houses in the compound of homes, barns, pens, equipment sheds and corrals. A handsome woman in plaid shirt and slacks opened the back door, arms full of pumpkins and acorn squash she had just brought to the back porch, preparation, she told me, for her daughter Julia's birthday dinner the next night, when a suckling pig would be roasted. Linda Davis told us to take off our boots and come in. The house was an adobe shell that had been added to over the years. Like the ranch itself, it merged the histories and personalities of two old New Mexico ranching families, the Springers and the Mitchells. Perhaps fifty feet long, the living room—with its cozy fireplace circle of sofas and chairs, cattle magazines and *National Geographics*, its racing trophies, books, maps, billiard and ping-pong tables, its bar and western art, Les Davis' beloved opera on the stereo and the lively talk of half a dozen handsome young adults—was as active a center of ranch family life as I would see. All six children either work with Les and Linda on the ranch, or—like Julia, a lawyer in Santa Fe—plan to return.

"You're not going anywhere tonight," Linda had announced, as we settled in for several hours of talking, sustained by a hearty home-grown meal. We were shown pictures of the huge dam Grandfather Springer had built across the headwaters of the Cimarron River, which the ranch controls, an Aswan-like project for a ranch to have undertaken, but, physically, its greatest strength. We studied maps of the 1,700,000-acre Beaubien, later the Maxwell, land grant, from which the CS had been carved, and listened to Les, a man of civilized interests, talk of the dramatic land grant litigation his grandfather Frank Springer had carried to the U.S. Supreme Court, and of the early Hereford herd Springer had brought to the CS in 1882. Springer also became a world authority on paleontology and geology. Linda's late father, Albert Mitchell, had run the great Bell Ranch to the southeast for years, headed almost every major cattle organization in the nation and been honored both in the Hall of Great Westerners in Oklahoma's Cowboy Hall of Fame and by the same Golden Spur award Watt Matthews had received. But ranching success had grown from struggle. As Linda spoke of her childhood at the western edge of the dust bowl, I could almost feel the stinging sandstorms that had blackened the sky and forced her father, Albert Mitchell, to ship and drive his herds hundreds of miles south into Mexico during the worst drought years from '33 to

John Brittingham repairs a windmill after an ice storm in the high plains east of Denver.

'35. I left convinced that if there is strength in family commitment and continuity, the future of the ranch may lie, as much as anywhere, with the CS in Cimarron.

On the high plains southeast of Denver, the winds blow the grass free of snow in the winter, letting John Brittingham's herd graze freely over 14,000 acres. But it tears across the exposed plains, sculpting and bending the tenacious scatter of pines, driving snow into drifts that trap cattle, isolating John for days from even his closest neighbor, Terry Kelsey. "The storms kill you. And then a calf is born," says John, with a tenderness that is tested constantly by the elements, "Last year, a longhorn bull leaped over a high barbed wire fence and roamed with the cows for five or six days. They'll go over anything. We knew we'd have some calves coming early. The first ones were born just this week." John's life, in this powerful, open landscape, is a series of violent swings from sophisticated activity to primitive confrontation. A nationally ranked glider pilot, he competes for the U.S. in international soaring meets. When the blizzards rage outside the rambling white ranch house that hugs the top of a lonely knoll, he turns classical music up to full volume and sits in his leather wing chair by a roaring fire surrounded by his western paintings and bronzes, his Navajo rugs and cowhides, his books and pewter, and revels in it. But the harshness of Colorado can cut him like a knife. "It started snowing this Christmas Eve. The wind picked up and drifted in fifteen-foot drifts around the house. The cattle were scattered all over, caught in the drifts. I worked all Christmas Day with my hired man to get the cattle out and fed. We lost two cows and a calf." But then he smiles wryly at the humor of the range. "One cow had packed down a four-foot-high ice platform, and every time she tried to get down, she'd plunge into snow up to her shoulders and would scramble back up. For four days, she never moved. When we finally dug her out and pushed her off, she went galloping off to find friends and water." John had felt the same need for contact after the storm. "The minute I could get out, I raced over to the Kelseys. But they'd done the same thing, and raced to town for food." I suspected that these wild alternations of the mood of ranch life were part of what led John Brittingham to say, "I am doing what I like best to do."

Alert now to the buckaroo, I was tempted to retrace the emigrant route west through southern Wyoming and the Continental

Ranch gate near Boulder, Colorado.

Divide to Salt Lake City, then across Utah and Nevada to California. I had made this trip before, through the range between Elko and Winnemucca, Nevada, where true buckaroos could still be found. It was land so wide, with ranches so large, that for miles the only exits off the freeway said simply "Ranch." But I wanted now to follow it as a drover or herder would, moving slowly over the Continental Divide, watching for the first creek and patches of grass near Coalville after the mountain canyons and resting there with relief, facing the Great Salt Lake, the desert sink of Nevada and the Sierra with dread, and dreaming of the paradisiacal grass of the California foothills.

Instead, I continued north through the great ranching belt that runs up the east side of the Rockies into Alberta, then drove west to the Cariboo, where my affection for ranches had begun. The closer I came to the Canadian border, the more similarities there seemed to be binding together the thousands of miles of range country I'd travelled. And yet each state had burned its individual brand on the ranches within it. This is powerfully true in Texas, but even more so in Wyoming, where you quickly learn that cattle and the creation of Wyoming are synonymous. Politics, history and grass are inseparable. The Oregon Trail and the Pacific Union Railway plied the state from east to west, both powerful shapers of history. The state was largely molded by the Wyoming Stock Growers Association; its presidents have become senators and governors, sat in Congress and Assembly, and still do. In many states and provinces, ranchers find themselves a political minority, threatened by government and dismissed as an insignificant economic force. But in Wyoming ranching is still more important financially than any other form of agriculture, and cattlemen still have high status.

Typically, the executive director of the Wyoming Stock Grow-

The grazing lands of the Padlock Ranch, straddling the Wyoming-Montana border.

ers, Dean Prosser, operates a big family ranch east of Cheyenne and has just returned to full-time cattle politics after two terms in the state Assembly. His office, a converted house close to the state capital, is just a few blocks away from where once stood the Cheyenne Club, the financial and social center of the western cattle business during the 1880s, when the fast-growing industry had attracted young men from New York and Boston, England and Scotland.

Even on the most contemporary Wyoming ranch, history overpowers the present. At first, the vast Padlock Ranch straddling the Wyoming-Montana border might seem aloof from the past. As ranches go, it is rather new, assembled in the 1940s and '50s by Homer Scott, who came to the area as a construction engineer, and now run by his son, Dan. The Padlock is a thoroughly modern ranch. Actively diversifying (diversification is another buzzword of the range, as ranchers seek to free themselves from total dependence on a shaky cattle market), the Padlock has developed its own coal mines, feedlot and extensive corn and hay operations. And yet it breathes tradition; the ranch still runs a horse-pulled chuckwagon on the summer range, a sight that has vanished on most ranches, where cowboys drive home at night in pickups. Two-thirds of its seventy-odd permanent employees are cowboys who ride a kingdom of grama grass rich enough to run a cow on just twenty-five acres. Its magnificent ranges in the Big Horn Mountains attract camera crews shooting Marlboro commercials. Above all, history pervades the Padlock. Much of the ranch lies within the Crow reservation on land leased from the tribe. Padlock cattle can be seen from a gentle hill that commands a 360-degree view of inestimable miles of rolling range. On the north flank of the hill are a group of plain white wooden crosses, one marking the spot where Colonel George Custer died. This land is now cattle country because of that single cross.

Shock and outrage at Custer's killing in 1876 by Sioux Chief Sitting Bull and his braves forced open the seductive grasslands of the Powder River Basin and the vast territory that rolls from north of the Platte River to east of the Bozeman Trail in southern Montana, lands that had previously been forbidden to ranchers because of treaties with the Indians. What followed was one of the most dramatic phases of North American ranching, the rise and fall of the open range, which began with Custer's death in 1876 and ended a brief 16 years later a hundred miles to the south with the Johnson County War in 1892.

A 60-mile-per-hour chinook wind thaws snow and bares grass, bringing the gift of winter grazing to northern Wyoming; but a freeze after the chinook thaw can leave a crust on the snow that cuts cows' feet like knives.

The steady cycle of the years and seasons at the Padlock make it hard to grasp the tumult of history this area has been host to. No sooner had the land been taken up and filled with cattle, and the Cheyenne Club built for the new cattle lords, than homesteaders began to pour in, encouraged by the federal government to settle and string up the just-invented barbed wire—the prickly strands that came to symbolize the farmer's threat to the rancher's free use of the range, for no longer could cattle graze freely. Although it had required huge annual roundups to sort out the mixture of brands and, with free-roaming bulls, had precluded scientific breeding, the open range embodied the idea of freedom that still clings to the cowboy. In 1886, blizzards destroyed herds, bankrupted ranches and brought many ranchers, already weakened by the encroachment of settlers, to their knees. As ranchers struggled to rebuild their herds, sheep moved in, overgrazing the range and setting up a new rivalry between the rancher and sheepman.

The frustrations of the rancher exploded in the Johnson County War, when a train load of heavily armed ranchers and gunmen organized by the Wyoming Stock Growers moved north to drive out rustlers and squatters who, they believed, were violating the ranchers' grazing rights. The bloody debacle that

Corrals and fences, Ridgeway, Colorado.

resulted focused national attention on the range. The abortive war, dramatically reported in eastern papers, aroused a storm of concern in Washington, but the ranchers were unable to forestall the inevitable, and the Johnson County War marked the end of a chapter in western history.

The Padlock looked big enough to have buckaroos. When I asked Dan Scott about them, he dismissed it with, "Ah, they're a highly mobile, flashy breed of itinerants who come around here and won't get off their horse." But he drove me thirty miles back from the nearest road to meet cowboy Jack Cooper at one of Padlock's camps. Cooper lives here with his wife, Dorothy, and those of his ten children who are still at home, punching cows as far away from the home ranch as he can get, tending single-handed a herd of several thousand cows and calves on a range of 15,000 acres. He's been cowboying long enough to have raised three sons who have become working cowboys. He pulled out some gear to show me—chink chaps with fringes, a hand-braided bridle with engraved silver Salinas mouthpiece made in Elko, Nevada, and the richly carved Visalia saddle with slick fork

Above: Log snake fence, British Columbia.
Below: State motto.

and deep seat he was rebuilding for his son. "I like that buckaroo equipment," Jack said. "I've heard say the closer you stay to the old Spanish style the better off you are, because they had the best." I must have looked as if I had found the lost tribe. Jack let out a whoop of laughter, and nodded, "I guess you'd call my style buckaroo."

In the Smith River Valley an hour's drive east of Helena, Montana, in foothills with an elevation too high and a growing season too short for anything but grass and cattle, I found Bob Hansen in the upstairs den of his new house, ranching with his TRS computer. He inherits 101 years of Hansen family ranching in the region, but he doesn't look to history to keep the Hansen Ranch healthy over the next decades. He is on line with Agrinet, a Nebraska-based agricultural computer network that links ranchers in five western states. He taught himself from a textbook. "You're charged by the hour. You pay by Visa card. I punch in data, and in four or five minutes I have the answer on my Mickey Mouse telephone." He's also hooked up to Compuserv, which for about $25 an hour allows him to get up-to-the-minute grain or cattle futures prices, scan the Washington *Post* news service or check the FAA weather briefing before he flies his Cessna to Bozeman. The computer has already saved cows. "We were having a problem finding the right ratio of chopped hay and grain for our first-year calves. They were bloating on us and dying. We called up Agrinet and found that the ratio we were using—two to one—was a death ratio."

He strokes an old buffalo robe his father-in-law used when driving teams during Prairie winters in Saskatchewan. "Fifteen years ago we were putting up hay with a team of horses. Now we've got swathers and bale stackers." He presses the Modum 1 button, then the Enter button, and within minutes Agrinet is telling him how to get the most weight gain on his calves for lowest cost. "You wonder how $1 million can run through your hands in a year, when, if you're lucky, all you're looking at in the end is $50,000. Most of the time you break even. We can do it because we're not mortgaged, and we're old." And they are on line with a TRS-80.

But in Montana, history and cattle economics seem insignificant in comparison to the power of the land and sky. As you stand in the grazing land near Two Dot, close to the center of the state, an ocean of cream-gold washing away to an ice blue range of mountains, distant cattle black silhouettes against the grass, the

Pole snake fence, British Columbia.

state's nickname, "Big Sky Country," no longer seems a cliché.

As if orchestrating a show for my passage, the sky was gathering up a spectacle as I drove north toward Alberta very early on my last morning in Montana. A wind was blowing so strongly that it set the wooden sign identifying this as the northernmost point of Lewis and Clark's explorations—a place dubbed Fort Disappointment—swinging so hard it was dizzying to read. But it felt like spring, not January. To the west, the sky looked as if it were heralding the end of the world or a new Messiah. It was almost white at the horizon, turning to an eerie pale yellow contained by a clean-edged arc of cloud, black-bottomed as coal, spanning the sky in a monumental parabola from north to south. The arc became blue-gray toward its top, and, as if shot from the thick cloud of the arc, a fast-moving sheet of thin cloud raced east, overtaking what had been innocent blue sky. I had seen the Chinook arch, the front of warm air that blows in from the Pacific, sending temperatures rocketing forty or fifty degrees in an hour, baring the grass so that cattle can graze in midwinter, and giving ranchers a rejuvenating break from the long winter. Chinooks also have their vicious side. When melted snow refreezes, it can create a crust that encases the grass and cuts the cows' feet. "But I live for the Chinook," a southern Alberta rancher's wife told me as she helped spread hay along the base of a fence so that cattle could push their heads through and eat—a chore that must be done daily, even in arctic cold.

In northern Montana, strips of plowed earth alternating with grain stubble ran up into the foothills, sliced off abruptly where the plow met range that was too rough or thin for planting.

The pride of a ranch can often be measured in the craftsmanship and condition of its corrals and fences. Here, a fine set of corrals at the OH Ranch near High River, Alberta.

There was not a strip farm to be seen on the Milk River Ridge in Alberta, home of the splendid old McIntyre Ranch; strip farms appeared to have ended at the border. The Canadian and American wests had been handed different histories. The earliest trickle of cattle into Canada's grasslands was not driven in from Texas but shipped in from England and eastern Canada to supply the Hudson's Bay Company's trading forts in Oregon territory, or trailed westward across the Prairies. And the style of early ranching had been profoundly different, for Canada had never had a lawless west, vigilantes or real Indian wars. The gun had never been part of a cowboy's basic gear—although the American cowboy's reliance on the gun has been distorted by books and movies. The Hudson's Bay Company had imposed its version of British law and order on the land long before it bcame cattle country, and the North West Mounted Police had confirmed the patterns.

And yet, when the Canadian grasslands began to fill in the late nineteenth century, it was American cattle and cowboys who flowed up from Montana, Oregon and Washington. Much later, in the 1960s, another wave of Americans bought ranches in B.C.

and Alberta, and have merged into the Canadian ranching scene. Most ranchers today are part of the international ranching network. The McIntyre's manager, Dr. Syd Slen, bought purebred Hereford bulls from Les Holden in Montana. In Lethbridge, range historian and range management specialist Alexander Johnston shared research with professors of range management at Berkeley and Ogden, Utah. At seminars of the Society for Range Management, Alberta foothills rancher Gordon Cartwright tramped the range identifying grasses with colleagues from all the northwestern states. From British Columbia's Nicola Valley in the south Cariboo, Douglas Lake Cattle Company's manager Joe Gardner flew to San Antonio for the International Stockmen's Foundation conference, kept the ranch's champion quarterhorse Peppy San—a half brother of the King Ranch's famous San Peppy—at stud in Texas and trucked foals back and forth across the border between Texas and B.C. And though Canadians often fear excess U.S. beef flooding the Canadian market, Alberta rancher John Cartwright says, "Everybody's been dinged by American beef at one time or another, but the whole story is that for every ten head they ship in, we ship 100 south. There's a *good* U.S.-Canada relationship in cattle. If the border stays open, it helps stabilize both markets. And we both have the same major problem: government interference!"

Ranchers have always sought out the same things: the creeks and springs, the good grass and temperate climate. With broad strokes, the Maker (as cowboys call him) created rangelands in a pattern that transcends artificial boundaries. Ranchers in the Cariboo and Mexico share, essentially, the same long strip of semiarid desert range. Grass is the basic bond, and climate the common determinant. From Kingsville, Texas to the Chilcotin, this contemporary network of breeding, range management, politics and computers ties ranchers into an even more tightly knit community.

I found Gordon Parke at Upper Hat Creek feeding his cattle from the back of a tractor-pulled wagon piled high with baled hay. Trying to keep his balance at the edge of the wagon as it bumped over snow-drifted pasture, he would slash the baling string with his knife and dump the bales on the ground, trying to satisfy the 100 or so cows that surged around the wagon, their breath steaming in the freezing air as they bawled and pushed with a frenzy that reminded me of the cattle drive. Apart from the method of hauling the hay, this job has not changed for 100 years. But disquieting change hung over the Cariboo. Gordon

Blacksmith shop, Eaton dude ranch.

told me that the Gang Ranch had gone into receivership. The Gang was 900 square miles of magnificent country eighty miles to the north, for more than 100 years one of British Columbia's best known ranches. For anyone who had grown up to the romantic ring of the name Gang Ranch, its collapse was as unimaginable as the collapse of the King Ranch would be to a Texan.

And yet, over time, ranches rise and fall, like empires. They are assembled and disassembled, bought and sold. Boundaries seldom stayed fixed. They are evolving, organic things. Gordon Parke and his brother had split the old Bonaparte in two at their father's death. In the few years since the cattle drive I had joined, Gordon had traded the leased summer range we'd conquered for a government grazing lease on the other side of Hat Creek Valley and, as he slashed the hay bales, the ranch faced the possibility of its most major surgery yet. Hat Creek sits on the deepest coal deposit in North America, and though the project was now on hold, the provincial power authority that owns the mineral rights could turn the east end of the valley into an open pit coal mine that would devastate both rangeland and the valley's established ranching culture. It was the same energy threat that hovered over Point Conception 2,000 miles south.

There was nothing inherently tragic in change. But beyond the crisis at the Gang was the larger question: Would beef itself survive the century? We had come to cattle country as meat eaters, but, given changing diet patterns and the needs of burgeoning populations for more efficient protein sources, might we even abandon our traditional food source?

But while these issues loomed, Gordon had to get the feeding done. "Hard work doesn't hurt you, but it *is* hard work," I remembered him saying the previous summer as he and his wife, Linda, had moved 40-foot lengths of irrigation pipe in an alfalfa pasture, a job that must be done each day on these fields that are too uneven and too irregular to use the easier roller irrigation. And yet they worked with a comforting backdrop of history; standing beside the hayfield was the silvered old log stopping house that had served a river of miners, mule trains and cattle that was flowing along the Cariboo Trail to the gold rush when Gordon's granduncle, Philip Parke, first planted his hay here in 1862.

I'd watched him brand, sitting on the calf held between the bars of a branding table, burning the PP brand into the hide in only four seconds. Cutting and roping, dragging and wrestling 100 calves through the wild assembly line of innoculations, ear tags, branding, castration and dehorning that would identify and protect them, and determine their destiny—breeding or slaughter—Gordon would end the day covered in blood, sweat and manure. Almost every day in the summer, he drove to a high lake to dig out a beaver dam that, with frustrating regularity, closed off the flow of water to one of his hayfields. Shovelling hard, up to his shins in mud, he laughed one day, "Sometimes I wonder why I don't just bail out."

But it was clear that he relished the richness and variety his way of life held, and the self-reliance it forges. He could handle life on a physical level that, for the rest of us, is just tribal memory. John Cartwright in Alberta had mused on the persisting power of the ranch. "It's funny," he said, "We have friends who make more in a week than we make in a year. But they envy us. With their big, fat incomes and expensive homes, they would like to be here."

Survival requires change. And as I drove back to California

The semiarid bunchgrass range of the famous Gang Ranch in British Columbia's Cariboo is the northernmost tip of the great desert belt that stretches up from central Mexico.

through the great range lands of Washington and Oregon, through the California sheep and cattle country of Red Bluff and Mendocino County I felt as powerful a need as ever for contact, however vicarious and transitory, with the space and beauty, the qualities and values of the ranch. The more I saw and learned, the more understanding I felt for the rancher I met in a coffee shop in Depuyer, Montana, a man who'd struggled with weather and grizzlies and wrapped ranch chores around an eight-hour-a-day job for thirty years to carve a ranch and build a herd up on land he didn't even own. George Denboer had sounded profoundly satisfied as he said, "If we get all six kids raised on the ranch, it don't make too much difference if we own it."

THE LAND

That basic axiom of ranching, "Whoever controls the water controls the land," still leads to water wars; today's battles among ranchers, states, nations and competing interests may be less bloody but no less intense than those of the past. Snaking through the desert range near Hatch in southern New Mexico, the Rio Grande has been a lifeline of the cattle industry since Onate first trailed cattle north into New Mexico in 1598.

Previous page: Though ranchers have historically hated farming, this rancher must dig to dam and divert the waters of his spring to flood a potential hayfield. This is valley mountain ranching in Pitkin County near Snowmass, Colorado.

The Bow River where it flows by the Goose Lake Cattle
Company ranch in southern Alberta.

The rule of thumb for ranchers is that cattle should never be more than a mile away from water. *Far Left:* At the Perry Minor Ranch near Bindloss, Alberta, springs have been dug out to create this brilliant blue gem. *Above:* The Padlock Ranch, with ranges sprawling over the Montana-Wyoming border, controls this waterhole in the Wolf Mountains.

The grandeur of the Shoshone Mountains in northwest Wyoming does not suggest the role of the mountains in the evolution of good ranching country: They are the source of the foothills soil that has eroded from the rock and washed down, giving range grasses something to take root in, and the source, too, of the river that has spilled fertile soil by its banks and provided irrigation water for hayfields and pasture.

Diversification is one of the means of survival for ranchers facing the marginal economics of beef raising. At the San Julian Rancho near Point Conception, California, diatomaceous earth is dug from land that cannot be grazed—a more profitable crop today than cattle.

Cattle still graze on this old Mexican land grant, the San Julian Rancho where 150 years ago vaqueros rode. The grass here grows so luxuriantly in the mild coastal climate that it fattens a cow on just ten acres. The seeds of strong annual grasses that sustain heavy grazing were carried in on the wool of sheep driven in from Mexico and the east by the Yankee sheepmen who followed the Spanish rancheros, changing the ecology of the range. Where perennials such as bunchgrass and grama dominate in most of the west's rangelands, this is filaree and burr clover country. Few of the great old ranchos that sprawled like feudal baronies up the California coast in the nineteenth century have been able to survive the insatiable desire of California's cities for more land.

The old Spanish rancho lands in the Santa Ynez Valley are now fenced into horse farms and weekend ranchettes that have become some of California's most valuable real estate. President Ronald Reagan's recreational ranch is nearby.

Overleaf: JA Ranch, Clarendon, Texas.

South of Choteau, Montana. Ranching country immortalized by A.B. Guthrie who lives nearby.

Summer range in the Big Horns.

Overleaf: New Mexico cattle country. Part of the continent's "hot desert," its rangelands are home to perennial grasses of southern origin.

Spring storm near Durango, Colorado. Better equipped
than cows to deal with harsh winters, horses can paw
their way through the snow to find food.

First storm of winter on a high plains ranch in Colorado.
Here the fierce winds bare the grass, letting the cows
graze year round. But for most ranchers in the snow belt,
a daily feeding of hay will be required to fatten the herd
through the winter.

South of Buffalo, Wyoming. Snow can be melted in hours by the warm winds of the chinook that several times a year soften the harshness of winter in western Canada and the more northerly American ranching states.

Overleaf: Early morning mist, the James Ranch near Durango, in southwestern Colorado.

Near Ridgeway, Colorado, July.

Though best known now as the name of shopping malls
and suburban subdivisions, the former great land grant
rancho, Mission Viejo in Orange County, California, still
clings to cattle ranching and leaves some of its grazing
land unplowed. Most, though, has given way to more
intensive agriculture or development.

In Alberta, as in Orange County, ranching and agriculture
abut here in the Neutral Hills in eastern Alberta where
ranching meets the Saskatchewan wheat belt. The oceans
of tall-standing native grasses that once grew as high as a
buffalo on the deep soils of the Canadian and American
prairies were, with the coming of the pioneer, the first to
be grazed down and plowed.

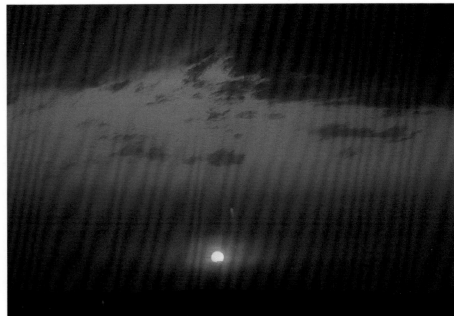

Duststorm over Texas Panhandle.

Full moon, New Mexico.

Caring for large bands of grazing sheep is still the lonely job of herders, who must protect the sheep from predators and keep them from overgrazing, which, in the past, led to deterioration of grasslands and to range wars between sheepmen and cattlemen. Able to live on less water and on rougher, sparser land than cattle, sheep graze here on a winter range on the arid buttes near Buffalo, Wyoming.

Summer range atop the Big Horn Mountains in northern Wyoming.

Overleaf: Monuments to loneliness, rock cairns like this one in the Shoshone Mountains were built by shepherds for entertainment or as markers. Over time, lichens and wildflowers have turned them into random rockery gardens of great charm. Sadly, now that remote ranges are accessible by four-wheel-drive trucks, many cairns are being dismantled and hauled away to decorate suburban gardens.

In spring, irrigated meadows and natural grassland combine to give park-like scenery at Douglas Lake, British Columbia.

To a rancher's eye, these scenic trees are invaders march-
ing into his grasslands, decreasing the cow-carrying
capacity of the range with every acre they overtake. These
classic grasslands have become a laboratory, part of the
range preservation and research program operated here
by the privately and publicly funded Research Ranch
near Fort Huachuca, Wyoming.

Alberta in June.

Ranch road in Alberta,
oiled to keep down dust.

Overleaf: Princes and poets have owned land alongside working ranchers in this southern Alberta landscape, all trying to live the dream of the western outdoor life.

Near Sheridan, Wyoming.

Hay—a rancher's gold
at the end of this
summer rainbow.

THE LAND

WHOEVER CONTROLS THE WATER controls the land," says Mike Curran, owner of the 40,000-acre Dearborn Ranches in the Montana foothills. He is in the midst of an all-out war with the state's Department of Fish and Wildlife and environmental groups, who want to make the spectacularly beautiful Dearborn River that flows through his ranch lands accessible to the public. An idyll of moody canyons, dancing rapids and deep pools, it is one of the best fishing and floating rivers in Montana. "Three years ago," Curran says, "floaters caused a fire that burned six square miles—4,000 acres. The public's lousy stewards!"

Ranching still outranks tourism as a source of state income in Montana, but tourism is rising fast. "What if, in a dry year, the state decides the best use of the water is fishing and floating rather than livestock and hay?" Curran asks. "Will the cattle have access to water? And will the state take over mineral rights in the creekbed? Oil and gas leases are one of our best 'crops' right now. Would they tear out our irrigation dams if they blocked the canoes? And who'll pay to move the fences that now run across the river?"

Range wars have always been fought over water, but the issue here is an even larger one. Now, as population presses out from urban centers, wanting room to play and live, needing water and power, competition for use of the open land builds from the California coast to the Maritimes; the entire North American rangeland has become a battleground. With empires of it still privately owned, more empires owned by and leased from the government, the issues of the Dearborn war arise wherever people and cattle coexist. "The public at large has no respect for the land," says fourth-generation rancher John Cartwright, near High River, Alberta, echoing Curran as he tries to keep hunters out when there's a high risk of fire. "We're in a conflict mode. The person who lives in a box in a city looks at all those acres and thinks you're being selfish. People oppose the right to own or control that much land. They don't know how many acres it takes to run a cow. Or what a fire can do to your winter hay."

On the land itself there is a struggle of a different sort for dominance and survival, one that has been going on since the first hollow-stem blade of needle grass appeared perhaps thirty million years ago. Cattle grazing benignly, single-mindedly searching out forage in their meadows, are oblivious to their role in the great drama of the rangelands, part of the process of evolution and great geologic events that have given birth to the largest area of natural grassland in the world. The Western Rangeland, as formally defined by a U.S. government study in 1930, encompasses half the North American continent; though scholars of the range debate its true boundaries, Dr. Harold Heady, professor of range management at Berkeley, sees it as everything that lies west of a line that cleaves the very center of the country, a line that runs from the southern tip of Texas at Brownsville north through the heart of Oklahoma and Kansas, and the eastern sides of Nebraska, and South and North Dakota. Within this realm, the grasslands have, over the ages, created their own boundaries, most of them drawn by climate.

The soils in which grasses would take hold and become the climax vegetation—that fragile state where the land reaches a balance of climate, soil and plants that is its highest natural state of productivity—evolved from several sources. The vast inland sea that filled the heart of the continent ninety to 200 million years ago subsided, leaving sedimentary rock that decomposed into the rich, deep soil of the prairies. The Rockies were taking shape forty million years ago, a source of soil that washed down to form foothills on both east and west watersheds, and that, on the east, flowed out farther and flattened into the high plains. Smaller mountain ranges formed along the west coast, catching the rain as it blew in from the Pacific, creating a dry desert belt between the coast and the Rockies that stretched, essentially, from Mexico to central British Columbia. The Rockies, too, caught westward moving rain, leaving a dry belt hugging its eastern flanks. In the northwest, lava ash spewed from a chain of volcanoes, forming rolling volcanic ranges that eroded to a surface of soil.

It might take fifty acres to fatten a cow on this dry desert range in New Mexico.

Vegetation evolved, with species of grasses, weeds, shrubs and trees thriving, dying and migrating under the determining forces of climate. From their origins in the tropics, the family of tall bluestem grasses migrated north and took hold in the steamy coastal prairie where the King Ranch now sits. They spread up into the deep-soil prairie belt through the east of Oklahoma, Kansas and Nebraska, where warm storms blowing up from the Gulf of Mexico mixed with cool air and dumped summer rains that sent the bluestem springing up to six and seven feet. The bluestem flourished, too, in a pocket of Nebraska, the Sand Hills, where the sandy soil held more moisture than the thinner, gravelly soils that were more typical of the grasslands. But as they moved north, the numbers of bluestem species declined.

The short grama grasses, too, moved up from the south and evolved as the climax grass over a great crescent of dry, warmer range curving form southern Nevada east and north through New Mexico, Texas and up into Montana, where they confronted bunchgrass. As grama inched eastward into the prairies, it coexisted with bluestem and buffalo grass. Like the bluestem, the number of grama species shrank as they moved north, from eight or ten in Texas to only one or two in Montana. From a northerly evolution, bunchgrass found its way into the gravelly soils of the more northerly mountains and foothills, standing in noble three-foot clumps in Alberta, B.C. and the northern states. A cold-climate grass, its strongholds remained in the north, and it only thrived farther south at higher elevations.

Climate created the zones of dominance for each grass, and described their limits. The great desert strip west of the Rockies split into two, a hot and a cold desert, with the two coming together in southern Nevada, near Las Vegas. Here, bunchgrass, the great grass of the cold desert, gave way to grama, the short, hard grass of the hot desert. The cold desert had winter rains and dry summers; grasses grew fast in the spring, and then went dormant, curing on their roots, like hay. The hot desert was dry in winter, rainy in summer. Standing uniquely apart from these epic events of the range, the California coast rejected the perennials that dominated elsewhere. There, the warm sun and mild, wet winters favored filaree, a broad-leafed annual of Mediterranean origin that abounds in California. Reseeding itself by seeds encased in wind-carried spears that children in California transform into miniature scissors in the spring, filaree is not a true grass at all.

The climax species did not evolve in isolation. They have always coexisted with other grasses—ricegrass, wheatgrass, fescue. They play a tug-of-war for dominance with sage, mesquite and chaparral that move in when they weaken, and with forest. In the pinon pine and juniper forests that cover thousands of square miles of rangeland in Colorado and New Mexico, the grasses growing at the trees' feet must fight for soil moisture and sun, with gramas in the warmer regions, and bunchgrass in the colder.

But a factor other than climate played a role in bringing the grasslands to their superb readiness for the arrival of cattle. The grama and, especially, buffalo grasses of the plains evolved under grazing, and were forced to develop survival strategies by the huge herds of buffalo, elk and antelope. These grasses lay flat along the ground, avoiding overgrazing. Confronted by the new cattle, the grasses would prove far more resistant than the sturdy-looking stands of bunchgrass, which had never been reached by the wild grazing herds.

The rangeland was an incomparable gift to the first pioneers, but despite the tall-standing bluestem in the prairies, it was not voluptuous. It was essentially dry. Its soils were thin, its plant

The hand of man shows on this forbidding landscape. The waters of the Animas Creek have been recruited to help carve the huge Ladder Ranch out of the sparse grassland and greasewood of southern New Mexico.

growth anything but lush. It could be parched by drought, assaulted by blizzards, invaded by poisonous larkspur, rip-gut, cactus and grass-smothering mesquite. But the grass, tall and short, hard and soft, swept from the arboreal forest of the Peace River and the timbered wildernesses of British Columbia's Chilcotin in the north to the heart of Mexico. Straddling the Rockies and spilling in golden waves to the California coast on the west and across the great plains east to the Missouri where it stood as high as a buffalo, it offered incomparable feasting for livestock.

The tall bluestem grasses growing on the good, deep soil of the prairies were replaced swiftly by corn and wheat which gave a higher yield per acre than cattle possibly could. It is easy to feel sentiment for a sight we'll never see. To the delicate moral question of right or wrong, New Mexico State University Professor Gary Donart bravely speculates, "Plowing the best grass-

93

lands? Whether it was the right choice, in the corn, soy and wheat belt, there was really no choice. We needed agricultural food production. By now, most of the land we can get water to has been cropped. But farther west it's a different story." He speaks of the less hospitable land, the ranges bypassed in the first waves of farming where ranching has taken hold. "The range-lands are the cradle of the cattle industry, where the cow and calf harvest a forage source that's not going to be used to grow anything else. Grasslands are still the easiest way to produce food for the animals that support the industry—much cheaper than irrigated pastures. And ranges perpetuate themselves." Providing, of course, they are allowed to.

But water, again, is the fundamental issue of the western range. Sitting in Las Cruces, the center of the El Paso-New Mexico groundwater battle that may well end in the U.S. Supreme Court, Donart says, "Before we learned to develop it, water was a limit to ranching, to cropping—to growth."

But water is far from inexhaustible. "We're sitting on a depleting water supply," Donart cautions. "If the groundwater goes, we may be out of water by the end of the century. Here, it could be the end of agriculture in the Rio Grande Valley." And then he adds a thought-provoking comment: "Perhaps any land that can't sustain itself on natural precipitation shouldn't be cropped or developed." It is a philosophy that could protect the range.

Ranching in the zone of impact of the Las Cruces water war, Rita and Janaloo Hill have watched the water table fall. "We bought the ghost town in '35 for the water rights. It's the springs here that brought the stagecoaches to Shakespeare, and the immigrant trails and cattle drives. We've got three wells for the cattle. But where water used to be at thirty feet, it's brackish now, and we had to go down to 145 feet with one of our wells, to the groundwater that took millions of years to accumulate!"

There is much to redress. "There was no concern for the ecology of the land. For seventy-five to 100 years, they operated in blissful ignorance," says Donart. "The Dustbowl and Texas Panhandle are pretty bleak now, but it was strong ranching country once. And east of Roswell, where grass should be as tall as a man, it's now sand dunes." Dr. Alex Johnston estimates that in the early 1970s seventy-five percent of the North American rangeland was still in only fair to poor condition, and believes that overstocking and overgrazing may have come from "a feeling, early in the century, that ranching was temporary in nature and that the land would soon be needed for farming, a

Irrigation canal near Montrose, Colorado.

feeling of uncertainty of tenure. The cattlemen and sheepmen resolved to get as much from the range as they possibly could. The range was characterized by camps rather than homes, men rather than families. The temporary and precarious nature of ranching discouraged scientific study, research and range restoration."

But now an army of ranchers, academics and government agronomists, bonded in both Canada and the U.S. by the Society for Range Management, has launched a dynamic effort to bring back the surviving range to at least a subclimax state, a mixture of great and lesser grasses and shrubs one level less productive than the climax state dominated by one grass. "There's stability in subclimax diversity," says Gordon Cartwright, John's brother, an eager member of the international network of men who talk the new language of the range, a language of invaders, increasers and decreasers, of manipulators and consumers. Gary Donart can be found standing over a small wire cage set up in the middle of New Mexican rangeland, comparing the ungrazed plants inside the cage with the grazed ones outside: his battlefield. It is a microworld of power plays between strength and weakness in which the successful grasses have accommodated to their conditions, exploiting the soil, moisture and the sun's energy with the adaptability that survival requires.

It has always been a precarious balance. For the best grasses are the most fragile, even a little lazy. They are the "decreasers" that, when overgrazed or waterstarved, lose their regenerative powers and die, opening the range to "increasers": tough, opportunistic plants that fill the vacuum but usually offer a little less food value. It's a Catch 22, for the tastiest climax grasses are eaten first, leaving the less palatable plants to replace them. In this ebb and flow of decreasers and increasers, the sunburst stands of rough fescue prized by foothills ranchers in Alberta and Montana give way to vetch and lupin, Indian rice grass yields to poisonous larkspur. Bunchgrass bows to sage, the aromatic dusty green shrub immortalized in western songs and paintings but which puts fewer pounds on a range steer than bunchgrass. Bunchgrass appears invulnerable, for each two- or three-foot-high clump stands clear of encroachment, on bare earth, the zone in which its deep and delicate root structure sucks all the available moisture and nutrients—the key to its drought resistance. And yet the tall grasses such as bunchgrass are more vulnerable than short grasses, for they are the first to be grazed and so lose their vital leaf surfaces, while the short or creeping grasses hiding at their base are spared, and may prevail.

But both increasers and decreasers withdraw before the "invaders," the aggressive plants that move in when the healthy balances have been disturbed. Trees can invade and overtake a range. Ants, beaver and deer play their roles, too, in the subtle ecosystem of the range. With the intrusion of the master manipulator, European man, millions of acres of range deteriorated to the verge of unusability. Overgrazed climax grass gave way to weeds and shrubs, then to annuals and to bare ground. Where grass had become sparse and soil was exposed, drought and wind destroyed the more vulnerable parts of the range, turning them to desert. Almost everywhere, range was reduced to a fraction of its productivity, and mesquite threatened to take over the west. Where the ranchers and cowboys of the 1880s saw barbed wire as the end of their freedom and culture, and still fight it in spirit, today's disciples of range management see barbed wire as the salvation of the range, for it gave birth to controlled grazing, reseeding experiments and systematic breeding programs.

A bend on Willow Creek, with the rich native bunchgrass of the Porcupine Hills complemented by water that would allow the cultivation of hay and a kitchen garden. The Allie Streeter Ranch near Nanton, Alberta.

Now, many strategies are being conceived, debated and tried. In New Mexico, stacks of gnarled pinon stumps attest to Gilbert Ortiz's efforts to fight back the pinon at Forked Lightning, the magnificent pink adobe ranch on the Pecos that he manages. As appealing as the dark, rounded shapes are against the pale gold grama grass, the scattered platoons of hundreds of infant pinon trees invading the grazing meadows for his Santa Gertrudis cattle suggest that his efforts are merely delaying tactics. At America's most famous ranch, the King in southeast Texas, the innocent copses of hackberry, oak and mesquite that sprinkled the lavish sea of native coastal bluestem and red grama grasses when Rio Grande steamboat captain Richard King first saw it in 1852 have grown to impenetrable brush jungles of mesquite and huisache. Bringing powerful weaponry to the endless battle, the ranch moves massive bulldozers into the mesquite, dragging plows eighteen inches below the surface to cut the brush off at the roots, then reseeding the cleared pastures with its own King Ranch-evolved bluestem grasses.

Summer hay drying on the TE Ranch in Cody, Wyoming.

And in the Rocky foothills in Alberta, Gordon Cartwright fights encroachment by aspen poplars that, every year, overtake enough grassland to carry ten cows—grassland Gordon has raised to a subclimax state, a vigorous potpourri of bunchgrass, rough fescue, Parry's oatgrass and a scattering of undesirable shrubs. "But without this diversity it would be susceptible to disease, fire, devastation," Cartwright explains. His case for being allowed to burn back the poplar is persuasive: "This grassland developed over centuries with natural fire and the Indians burning it off. That's the established ecology. We can *choose* fire conditions that won't create erosion. And if we don't do controlled burning, it's only a matter of time—twenty, thirty years—before this country will light up, with a heck of a wind, and there'll be no stopping it."

Though only old-timers remember it, every rancher on the east slope of the Rockies feels the effects of the wild fire of 1910 that swept from northern Idaho almost to Calgary, driving elk before it, and creating after it new ground cover in which the elk thrived. They have now grown to herds of such size that they are a greater nuisance to the rancher than the coyotes and wolves that kill his calves. The proliferation is felt as far south as Helena, Montana, where Bob Hansen, who never saw an elk as a boy, watches them roaming in herds of 300 or 400 like marauding vandals, knocking down fences, attacking haystacks and competing with the cattle for grass. Although some ranchers create wildlife refuges on their range, many who suffer the predations of elk, coyote, wolf and grizzly—and of ravens and eagles, which can pluck the eye from a newborn calf—rejoice when their numbers are reduced by hunters. Like Mike Curran at the Dearborn, they often find themselves at odds with environmentalists.

Contact with this contemporary new language and ethic of the range gave me a new range consciousness: a rancher's eye. Instead of interpreting land in terms of form, color and texture, I began to look for a row of willow running through a semiarid valley with a drover's anxiety, for the trees trace a stream. And cows must be kept within a mile of water. The thrill of seeing a herd of white-tailed mule deer flashing up a bluff on the McIntyre Ranch in Alberta or the Lambshead in Texas was tempered with concern that cattle and deer compete for forage. Invasions of infant fir and pinon arouse a partisan feeling for the grasses under siege. And grass grazed down to dust on one side of a fence and standing in sturdy clumps on the other speaks of abuse versus responsible range management.

There is another facet of ranch land that even a trained eye cannot see: the subtle process of assembling the land. For old ranching families, there is the deepest kind of pride in having assembled, hung onto and continued to improve a good, self-sufficient working ranch. Gordon Cartwright revels in the saga of building the package of land, water and cattle that is now the Cartwright Ranches, thirty-eight sections of land, both deeded and leased from the government. Its 25,000-plus acres make it a middle-sized ranch that carries a herd of about 800 breeding cows. It is a textbook example of ranch-building over generations, a process of grasping opportunity and taking risks with a clear and patient eye on the goal of creating a self-sustaining ranching unit.

The Cartwright's was an eighty-year process of assembly that began in 1880, with grandfather Aubrey Cartwright catching ranch fever. "The first cattle had come through here in 1877, wintered successfully, and the word flew back east, 'Good water and grass!'" Gordon recounts. "Grandfather was studying law, having eye trouble, and was attracted to the newness of it all. He saw the land and was drawn to it because, as he said, 'A plow would never be set to it.'" The ranch began with the log cabin that now sits on Gordon's D Ranch, though at the time it was not his grandfather's, but a cabin built in 1889 by John Thorpe for the Bar U Ranch. The Bar U was one of the ranches that swiftly grew to a vast size in the early 1880s by accumulating land offered on 21-year leases at one cent per acre. Created by Fred Stimson, and the greatest of its time in the High River area, the

Bar U shared 100-cowboy roundups with neighboring ranchers—vast communal sweeps of the open range over several thousand square miles that, yearly, sorted out the mixed herds. It became a training ground for apprentice cowboys and hopeful young ranchers like Aubrey Cartwright. "Grandfather worked Bar U in the summer of 1900, and for Gordon McConnell who had a little ranch two and a half miles from here at McConnell Flats. In December of 1900, McConnell and Jack Nichol took advantage of a chinook to go to High River for supplies. The chinook thawed and flooded Stimson Creek, blocking their return, a blizzard overtook them, and they both perished." Violence and tragedy often collaborated in the process. Acquiring the McConnell ranch, Aubrey Cartwright and Thorpe became partners, picking up other parcels through the years, and Aubrey acquired his first brand—the D brand now used by Gordon—and 300 head of cattle that were the beginnings of his first commercial herd. "The D herd was basically the survivors of the hard winter of 1906-07, which forced Mike Herman to sell both the herd and the brand. He'd acquired the brand from Bob Dixon, who had gone insane."

Grazing land was building up, but they needed hayfields, a source for winter feed. Then as now, "young growing stock, and even some cows up to four years old, have to be carried over on winter feed. After that, they make it on the winter range." In 1914, they bought the Chain Lakes cow camp; it was some distance away, but its water for irrigated pasture made it the vital hay source. Here, and elsewhere, they could have bought mineral rights, too, "but at the time, it would have been more expense, and Grandfather and Father were more focused on trying to make this an economic operation." The preoccupation with building a good ranch passed from founder to son. For the next forty years, more parcels were added to the Cartwright holdings, "consisting mostly," Gordon says, "of homesteads that were too small—uneconomic—when the going got rough. The Cameron outfit never recovered from the disastrous winter of 1919-20. This place, where the D is now headquartered, was acquired in '26, with 300 head of cattle. So were the Roach and Nash homesteads, in the same year."

Virtually every large ranch has on it remnants of failed homesteads, victims, often, of an impossible dream (one fanned by the federal government in the early years) of farming profitably on acreages too small or on rangeland with soil too thin and rocky to sustain crops. The abandoned log huts and corrals are a moving sight, reminders of stoic effort and disappointment, of children and young mothers buried under anonymous wooden crosses, of the good humor and neighborliness that helped soften the hunger, cold and desperation of which the diaries of so many homesteading women speak so poignantly.

"My father added the old George Emerson homestead with some of the Bar U in 1950, when the Burns Ranches sold the Bar U off in parcels." The Cartwrights made the Bar U's HL Ranch their new hay source when their pastures at the Chain Lakes ranch were submerged by a reservoir. "What Dad envisaged was building up the physical base to carry on." In 1962, he had added the vital piece to the mosaic: the EP Ranching Company, owned by Edward, Prince of Wales, later Duke of Windsor, a ranch he had bought in 1919 after a visit to the area as George Lane's guest at the Bar U. The duke had joined the rush of young Englishmen eager to participate, often as absentee owners, in the glamor and adventure of a western "ranche." "With the duke in England, the EP had suffered," Gordon admits. "A lot of the good land was under willow. Several of the magnificent set of barns had burned down. But it looked good to us." It would give the Cartwrights, at last, their winter feed base close by. They could sell off the HL. "And with the EP, the ranch would be formed into a single block of land." The EP Ranch came up for sale in February '62. A chinook had all but washed out the bridge, making access to the sale difficult. But the Cartwrights were there. Inheriting an historic shrine, the duke's ranch house, has proved to be more nuisance than boon, for tourists come and visit, bringing litter and the threat of fires. But the Cartwrights handle it with grace. For they have the land.

There may be no more satisfying assemblage of land in the west than the Douglas Lake Cattle Company's in the south Cariboo. Flying over the watershed of the Nicola River—a great plateau of forest, lakes and grassland, ranch manager Joe Gardner can say the thing we all dream of being able to say: "Everything you can see is ours. Douglas Lake Cattle Company controls the grazing on all of it." Searching for cattle hidden in this expanse, he and his cowboss, Mike Ferguson, skim trees, turn tight on a wingtip to explore the gulleys and scan the half-million-acre range that is their turf. Seventy thousand acres is deeded land; the rest is leased. Over the hundreds of square miles that stretch out below them, the runoff gathers up and trickles into the Nicola, swelling it as it flows northeast to tumble into the Thompson, the green-blue river that runs, in turn, into the Fraser, which flows wide and powerful to the Pacific Ocean. Their range runs from the ridgelines of the crescent of snowy mountains that flank them to the east, south and southwest, to the graceful hills, hay pastures and small lakes round the home ranch on the banks of Douglas Lake to the north. It is land of such diverse climate and elevation that the cowboys can chase spring up to the higher elevations as they trail the cattle up to the spring ranges in April. At the northern tip of the cold desert that sweeps through the western states from southern Nevada, it is a surprise to find cactus and sage in land more known for its cold, snowy winters. It is game-filled country that sustains a full-time trapper, and a land of lakes. The meadows are crisscrossed with moose tracks; banking into a steep dive, Mike and Joe spot several browsing by a marsh-rimmed lake.

It is this almost magical conjunction of elements that makes Douglas Lake, as Nina Woolliams, wife of a former manager, said in her book, *Cattle Ranch*, "not just Canada's largest ranch, but one of the world's greatest. For the watershed possesses all the geographic features necessary for cattle ranching—spring, summer and fall range, flat land for cultivation, and abundant water." "We get first crack at the water," Joe yells over the noisy engine. "The ranch controls the headwaters of the Nicola, and owns all the deeded land along the river that could compete for the water." They overfly an abandoned homestead decaying back into the forest from which it had been hacked, one of the 100 little ranches bought up since the first homesteader came in 1872 to secure the Nicola's waters, and to build a balanced package of range, hay and water. This assemblage has been consolidated into four separate ranches, each with its own buildings, corrals and staff.

Grass, ultimately, is the key. The Cessna wings over the largest expanse of natural grassland meadow in British Columbia, huge tracts of grass kept free of trees at the lower elevations by lack of soil moisture. Fattening on the legacy of "a grass resource that's been well managed for thirty to forty years," as Joe describes it, Douglas Lake's cattle graze a species of bunchgrass, that is in such good condition that, even in semi-desert dry enough to grow prickly pear cactus, it takes just twenty-five acres to graze a cow. Climate cooperates. Tall clumps of bunchgrass bristle through the snow, texturing the hills. Climate cooperates. "You can see the grass in December. Our main cow herd of 6,000 cows is still grazing. It always bares off at this time of year, saving fifty tons of hay a day—$5,000 a day!"

As a cowman, Mike is one of the west's certified living legends, able to recall a cow's life history, keep the precise number of weaned heifers or yearling steers in his head at any given time and tell if a cow is ready to calve by the look in her eye. But as he talks about the grass, it's clear that protecting his herd's basic food source is as fierce a passion. It's the grass that keeps him from having his cows artificially inseminated, as so many ranchers do. "I don't like it, because you have to keep the cows close where you can see when they cycle, and that overgrazes the grass. I'll have 6,300 head of females with bulls this spring, when the new grass is most critical, and that's a hell of a lot of grass grazed down if you had to keep them all where you could see them. I keep them moving. I don't want it all chewed out." As Mike points out the new grainfield on a hill behind the home ranch, Joe chuckles, "He would have said no three years ago. Cowboys never have liked farming. He didn't want to lose an inch of his precious grass." But now Mike delights in the self-sufficiency they gain in growing their own grain. It is part of the diversification Joe has been initiating to try to overcome a bad cattle market, now at a four-year low. "I'm a diversification nut," he says, pointing out his timber operation. By milling its own fencepoles and lumber, selling timber, raising Christmas trees and selling feed supplements to neighboring ranchers, the ranch is trying to keep ahead of the tightening economic lasso. With a wintering herd of 11,000 head, Douglas Lake has found the healthy balance between cattle and available feed. Looking ahead to the year 2000, Joe says, "We could double the size of our herd if we could increase the productivity of our hay pastures with intensive irrigation." But that takes money. "And we have no dipping pot. The ranch has to pay its way," he says, a surprise to those who might assume that owner Charles W.N. ("Chunky") Woodward, chairman of the chain of Woodward's department stores, subsidizes the ranch, if necessary. Sharing the same recreational pressures Mike Curran feels on the Dearborn, and watching profits drop as recreational value of the land soars, Joe marvels, "Smaller ranchers would be tempted to sell homesites by the lakes, but Chunky has kept its physical integrity. It's *intact*!" As he and Mike snap on the Cessna's quilted winter overcoat on the runway above the home ranch, he adds, "Cutting off part of a ranch is like amputating fingers. It's never whole again."

THE LEGACY

The Barber Watkins Reynolds house, built in 1876, one of several stone ranch houses preserved on Lambshead Ranch, a working ranch that is also a rare museum of west Texas ranch architecture and history. In 1980, the lower floor of the house was flooded shoulder deep when the Clear Fork of the Brazos overflowed. In the year it was built, the house was the scene of the wedding of Sallie Ann Reynolds to John Alexander Matthews, one of the many weddings between the two pioneer families that have woven them into one.

Although famous in other states as a blazer of heroic cattle trails, Charles Goodnight is best known in Texas as the co-founder, in 1876, of the first permanent ranch in the Panhandle—the JA Ranch. The JA brand derives from Irishman John Adair, Goodnight's partner, who financed the ranch. The JA's first cattle were driven down from the Texas plains along old Comanche trails into the spectacular Palo Duro Canyon, a rancher's dream of protected grazing, where the Palo Duro Creek provided water, and opulent grasslands carpeted the valley that sat 1,000 feet below the plains.

Top left: This historic assemblage of buildings on the original JA Ranch is still owned and occupied by descendants of John Adair, founding partner. Running its Herefords on close to 200,000 acres, the ranch is now only one-fifth of its original size.

Left: The JA cookhouse, still in use.

Right: To a rancher, the beauty of the old Gardner home ranch near High River, Alberta, lies as much in its water source, its hayfields and high summer range as in its magnificent setting in the foothills of the Rockies.

Lower Right: Cattle grazing near the great ranchhouse at the historic 6666 in Guthrie, Texas.

Upper left: The Gang Ranch cookhouse, the heart of one of British Columbia's most famous ranches.

Left: This log house was Buffalo Bill's home in his later years. It sits on the TE Ranch on the south fork of the Shoshone River near Cody, Wyoming.

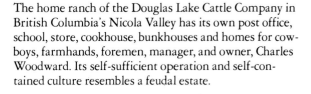

Cowboys and Indians, ranch wives and visitors, shop at
the Douglas Lake Cattle Company's store.

The home ranch of the Douglas Lake Cattle Company in
British Columbia's Nicola Valley has its own post office,
school, store, cookhouse, bunkhouses and homes for cowboys, farmhands, foremen, manager, and owner, Charles
Woodward. Its self-sufficient operation and self-contained culture resembles a feudal estate.

Old stable with hayloft near Ucross in northern Wyoming.

Outside the camp that is his home for several months on the high-elevation summer range, a British Columbia cowboy attends to the needs of his horse.

Buford, Colorado.

Machines and buildings are well maintained and painted at the OH ranch, Bert Sheppard's very traditional operation near High River, Alberta.

This handsome ranch house is at the Circle Diamond in
Picacho, N.M., part of the southwest ranching empire of
Robert O. Anderson. It is a replica, built from the original
plans, of the 1850s Baca house that stood in Las Vegas,
N.M., and is a fusion of rancho and Mississippi styles.

Corner of the living room in a ranchhouse on the Ladder
Ranch, near Truth or Consequences, New Mexico.

In a vacation ranch house in Colorado, the owners have created the western dream. The decor reflects the confluence of southwest desert and northern mountain ranching motifs, materials and traditions.

In a quiet parlor in the oldest adobe wing of the ranch house of the CS Ranch near Cimarron, New Mexico, the Les Davis family photographs are gathered. Inheritors of a distinguished ranching history, five of the six Davis children are actively involved in the ranch.

Carried over mountains, across prairies, round the Horn by ship, the piano was a symbol of civilized culture on the rough frontier. This one is at the Pitchfork Ranch, Meeteetse, Wyoming.

Above: Hand-plaited horsehair bridles and reins, a
virtually vanished art of the range, at the Sentinel Ranch.

Sentinel Ranch in San Patricio, New Mexico.

This ranchhouse at San Julian Rancho on the central California coast is a precious link with the rancho era that flourished on California's grasslands in the first half of the nineteenth century. It is still owned by blood heirs of the Spanish aristocrat Jose de la Guerra y Noriega, commandant of the military presidio at Santa Barbara, who was granted the land in 1837 to supply beef for the presidio and the mission at Santa Barbara. Infusions of Yankee blood from the east show in the wood sheathing of the original adobe, in the New England style and feel of many of the furnishings, and in the white picket fence that surrounds the casa and its charming garden.

The dining room, or *comedor*, of San Julian's casa, where the ranchero and his family dined at an authentic Chippendale table with matching chairs. The thickness of the original adobe brick walls can be seen at the doorway.

The sala at San Julian. Natural stone floors, spacious scale and white walls created the cool tranquility of rancho interiors. Here, as throughout the house, the cosmopolitan treasures gleaned from Santa Barbara's trading port are a melange from England, China, South America, the Philippines and New England. Out of respect for the geological faults that underly this region, the sala's grandfather clock is wired to the wall.

In a characteristic gesture, Dibblee Poett, courtly heir to the de la Guerra domains and heritage raises his hat to young visitors as he walks the long *corridor* of the casa. Basic to rancho architecture, the *corridor* has been embellished, over the years with neoclassical columns. At San Julian, Poett strives to maintain a small cattle herd and preserve the spirit of rancho life as well as the historic buildings.

Modernizing the region's indigenous adobe with bright pink paint and metal fences gives the Forked Lightning a certain stage-set beauty. The ranch owned by movie star Greer Garson and her husband, E.E. Fogelson, borders the New Mexican town of Pecos. *Top:* Forked Lightning's gate posts display the ranch's brand. Purebred Santa Gertrudis cattle graze the abundant pinon-dotted grass. *Above:* A decorative wall suggests the weathered adobe of early Spanish missions where cattle were raised in this northerly part of New Mexico as early as the mid-sixteenth century. *Right:* Native sage beside the buttressed ranch wall at Forked Lightning.

Corrals near Patagonia, New Mexico.

New wooden gates at the Douglas Lake Cattle Company
in British Columbia.

Above: A wreath of barbed wire, sage and leather greets Christmas visitors to the Mariposa Ranch near Cody, Wyoming.

Left: Barbed-wire fences were a transforming force in the 1880s, when they ended the roaming of cattle and cowboys over the open range, and gave birth to modern range management.

Discarded baling wire.

Pickups: part of the scene and part of the scenery.

Work horses bred in Detroit perform many of the chores on the ranch today. Rusted and dented, the cowboy's own favorites are often kept going with spares salvaged from derelicts.

The signs of ranch country; identification, decoration, and sometimes target.

Post office in Buford, Colorado.

Near Mora, New Mexico.

Discarded horseshoes at the Eaton dude ranch, Wolf, Wyoming.

The organic architecture of the range: a bunkerlike
Montana root cellar, essential for food storage before
electricity and refrigeration.

Sheep shed near Choteau, Montana.

The interior of the old stable on the Perry Minor Ranch near Bindloss, Alberta. Minor's grandfather came from the Sand Hills of Nebraska looking for sand hills in Canada that could shelter cattle in winter.

The Minors built this sod-roofed stable of escaped logs from a logjam in the Red Deer River.

"One thing cowboys love to do is rope—anything!" says cowboy Jack Cooper, who practises with his cowboy sons on this home-made cow that sits in the front yard of his home.

141

This cookhouse, more function than form, is in a cow
camp many miles from the headquarters of the Padlock
Ranch in Montana.

The propane lamp and stove are virtually the only
modern conveniences that have been added.

A classic cookhouse on the 100-year-old Pitchfork Ranch
in west Texas.

Scale of the huge pots and ladles suggest the numbers
that are fed from the Pitchfork's cookhouse kitchen.

Sentinel Ranch, San Patricio, New Mexico: Native adobe and the Spanish courtyard are combined in the ranch-house. Characteristic of old ranchhouses in the southwest and California, its wings have been built onto a simple rectangular adobe shell.

An early, primitive dugout of rock and adobe at the Sentinel Ranch. Dugouts were fast and cheap to build, and kept warm and cool by natural insulation.

146

Mexican artifacts and a handsome grain storage chest in the open-air *corridor* of the Sentinel ranchhouse.

A whimsical carved sunburst, in fact a *debujo*, or demon face, has been carved into the kitchen table top by the Sentinel's owner, the distinguished artist Peter Hurd.

Galleried in the grand manner, the two-story house on the Salman Ranch retains its rancho dignity and architectural purity in an enviable setting in the Sangre de Cristo mountains near Mora, New Mexico. It was built in 1863 on land of the original Mora land grant.

The tiny town of Watrous, New Mexico, was named for the man who built this exquisitely preserved dwelling, its adobe base enhanced by New England detailing. It is now the main ranchhouse of the Doolittle Ranch.

Intermarriage of the Spanish de la Guerras with the New
England Dibblees gave the casa at Rancho San Julian a
New England façade, which shows in the shingling, the
neoclassical columns and the picket fence. Over generations, the central and right wings were added to the
original wing, on the left, which began in 1805 as a
simple adobe shelter for travelling priests and soldiers
from the nearby Santa Barbara mission and presidio.

The utilitarian beauty of this old adobe tack room on the CS Ranch near Cimarron, New Mexico has evolved over generations. *Above:* Exterior. *Left:* Interior.

The porch of the bunk-house and cookhouse of the OW Ranch, Decker, Montana.

Tombstone, Galisteo,
New Mexico.

THE LEGACY

THE ONLY LIGHT AT LAMBSHEAD was a full moon. Shapes—low buildings, fences, trees—emerged from the flat compound I had reached with relief after a long and lonely drive in on a west Texas ranch road. The eighty-four-year-old lord of Lambshead, Watt Matthews was away, though he had assured me I was welcome to stay, and his cook and cowboys were asleep. The trees creaked and sighed in the wind. It was a place and a night for ghosts. I opened the front door of the first house I saw and found lights, beds, food and an inviting bookcase.

Among the books was *Interwoven: A Pioneer Chronicle*, the story of Lambshead told by Watt's mother, Sallie Reynolds Matthews. She had been born at the start of the Civil War of southern parents who had settled in west Texas. I read it through the night, enthralled. The 50,000 acres that spread out around me in the darkness were a microcosm of Texas and, in many ways, the west's ranching history. If not the birthplace, Texas had certainly been the nursery of the American cattle industry, and Lambshead had been on the main trail of the cattle culture as it fanned out from Texas after the Civil War. The people who had lived and died here had been touched by the powerful movements of pioneer America.

Sitting at Lambshead and listening to the wind, I was with Sallie's mother as she spent her first night on the prairies of west Texas. "All my life I had been accustomed to hearing the sound of axes, and the merry songs of the colored race, but there was no sound to greet my ears but the howling of wolves." On the southern fringes of the Panhandle, just west and north of Fort Worth, they had faced "a fine country for men and dogs, but hell for women and horses.... A synonym for lawlessness, desperadoes...a haven for lawbreakers from other states." But even though her own family would produce an outlaw, Sallie and her family seemed always to look for "a leaven of good...in this conglomerate mass of humanity."

Next morning I toured the ranch to see the country where this southern couple, Watt Matthews's grandparents, had come to bring up their children "outside of civilization, as it were." From gentle promontories in the rolling pecan and mesquite-dotted grasslands, I could see the Reynolds, Matthews and Bartholomew family houses that Watt and his family have preserved and restored. Though largely stripped now of the outbuildings and corrals that surrounded them when they were lively ranch headquarters, these old buildings have survived fire, time and the flooding of the Clear Fork of the Brazos, on whose banks they were built. They are solid, substantial two-story houses built of hand-hewn blocks of pink-beige local stone.

But Sallie's words show that during the early years, stability was an illusion. She had been raised in the transient existence that characterized the early cattle culture. Far from settling his family in one solid stone home for life, her father dragged the household, which at times numbered fifteen, from farm to ranch, from county to county, from Texas to Colorado and back again, sometimes selling at a sacrifice to move on. He, the other men, and sometimes the women, trailed cattle in all directions, from California to Kansas. "The life of these early settlers was a nomadic sort, for in those days no one owned any land," Sallie recalled. "The country was a virgin wilderness with plenty of lush grass, and the rancher moved his herd at will when he felt the need for fresh pasture. He would select a spot that looked promising, where he would build a cabin, tarry for awhile, then move on a good bit like Abraham and Lot of old.... Later, when the grass had come again, some other rancher would come along and occupy the deserted cabin. There were no permanent homes. One reason for this was the scarcity of building materials. Another was the proximity of Indians. No one knew when he might be molested and have to flee for his life."

The Civil War had made that fear a terrifying reality for the women. With many of the men pulled east to the war, the women huddled for protection in Fort Davis, which stood just over the county line from Lambshead and shared the same river, the Clear Fork of the Brazos. It, like Fort Griffin, which would be built later by the North on Lambshead's borders and which is now the home of the state herd of Texas longhorns, was one of the string of forts built to protect the scattered and isolated pioneer ranching families. At the fort, southern women, some of whom had brought their own slaves, learned neighborliness and self-sufficiency. "As we had no corner store to which to go when supplies ran low, three or four men would take their teams and drive to Weatherford, a round tip of two hundred miles, and bring back supplies for all." But they could buy no cloth; the war had blockaded the mills in the North. "The women were carding, spinning and weaving every bit of the cloth for all the clothing worn, making it by hand, as a sewing machine was unheard of in this country. My brothers were fond of hunting and had learned to tan the skins of the deer and antelope. From these, Mother made suits for the boys, thus saving herself a lot of weaving. When dozens of buffalo were killed at the ranch, Mother would take her scissors and go cut the long forelock, or mops as we called them, from the buffaloes' heads, enough to make a mattress, and a nice soft one it was." Young wives scarcely more than children themselves delivered one another's babies. The women molded candles, and made all their own soap.

And they learned to make their own fun. "In spite of war and dread of Indians...there was always feasting and dancing at weddings. It was no trouble to get up an old-fashioned square dance; fiddlers would play all night.... The women had quilting parties and were joined by the men when eating time came, and often the young men would sit around the quilt talking to the girls. There were candy pulls...made of molasses in a wash pot out in the yard." The two families, the Reynolds and the Matthews—all southerners who had been nearest neighbors from their first days in west Texas—kept the region lively with an endless string of weddings between the families. Everyone in the area was invited to the celebration that followed each wedding. For one, "there were seventy-five chickens killed beside other meat, turkey and boiled hams, pies by the dozen...and cake, cake, cake." A faded wedding certificate on the parlor wall of the Barber Watkins Reynolds house commemorates Sallie's own wedding in her father's house on Christmas Day, 1876, for which, even in this outpost, Sallie and her sisters threw themselves into a frenzy of dressmaking from the patterns printed in every treasured issue of *Harper's Bazaar.*

The festivities were enjoyed despite the threats and hazards of frontier life. "Once there was a dance, and some of the young men who had ridden from neighboring ranches had tied their horses near the house on the bank of the Clear Fork. When they went out to get their mounts, they were gone. In the morning, when daylight came, it was discovered there had been another dance under the river bank nearby, for the soft earth had been patted down by moccasined feet. They had danced before taking the horses."

Lambshead shared the very beginnings of the great expansion of the cattle culture north, east and west out of Texas. When the war was over in 1865, "the poor, worn, defeated soldiers of the Southern army began to return." They came home ready to hunt for new markets, and men and cattle began to move. In 1865, even before Sallie and her family had returned from Fort Davis, her brother was on the trail, driving twenty-five head of his cattle to Mexico. "But they learned that cattle were not selling well there, so they changed their course and headed for New Mexico. They sold their beeves at Santa Fe for a handsome profit...the first herd every driven from our part of Texas all the way through to Santa Fe." During the twenty years after the Civil War, Sallie's family joined drives to California, the most favored goal, for the cattle brought "fabulous prices," and were usually paid for in cash and gold—bags of gold. Their cattle flowed over the Chisholm Trail, which pushed over seven million head of cattle across the Red River, through Oklahoma to railheads at Abilene and Dodge City, Kansas. Their herds joined those of the leading cattlemen of Texas, Charles Goodnight and Oliver Loving.

A tragic outcome of one drive with herds from the XIT, a great Panhandle ranch, the largest in Texas at one time, was summed up in the terse telegram sent by Phin Reynolds: "A snowstorm struck us on the high divide fifty miles east of Denver, Colorado. Twenty-eight head of horses frozen to death. Six herds in one and drifted thirty miles south...Men all accounted for."

Through this era, as Sallie wrote, there were "no fences, everything was open range...and the annual round-up in the spring was the event of the year...a spectacular affair. Imagine several thousand cattle brought together on the open prairie with rolling hills for a background, men weaving in and out of the vast herd, each separating his brand. The man whose range it was would have his mess wagon and cook, perhaps two.... They would butcher a beef. There would be great pots of coffee, ribs broiling on spits before the fire, and the bread would be fresh baked in Dutch ovens.... Then each man would drive his cut back to his own range."

"The big drives were all over by the 1880s," says Watt Matthews, who was born in 1899. His first recollection was of a gentler side of ranching: the cowboy camp, where families gathered up into cavalcades of wagons and cowboys as they travelled great distances to tent together, visit and go to prayer meetings together.

There was need of faith and these reaffirmations of "the leaven of good," for, as Sallie emphasizes, "there was no law or order in the country...and these old cattle trails are marked by many graves." When the family first moved to the old Stone Ranch, a vacated homestead on the Clear Fork, the children searched mounds of rock for the abandoned treasures that were so precious to the pioneer—china, cowbells, ox yokes, furniture—and one day found a tiny coffin. "Of course it was immediately replaced as found," Sallie tells us, "and the little mound is still there." In the family cemetery at Lambshead, I stood before the grave of Sallie's little daughter, Annie, and felt some of the heartbreak in her words, "No one who has not passed through the same sorrow can possibly know the anguish of parting with a child.... She was laid under the daisies on the hillside near my father's home where she was born and where she died. The sun went under a cloud, the earth turned gray to me." But there was a new baby, and there would be more. "Life must go on, though hearts are breaking."

In Lambshead's old houses, objects of high civilization share space with the humbler homemade wooden water pitchers, rawhide-thonged chairs and back-porch cisterns. A sideboard holds flower-sprigged Spode china. Sallie's little cottage organ, "the first keyboard instrument in the county," stands in the parlor of her father's house. A gift from her father in 1875, it had been "one of the most wonderful surprises of my life. I do not believe a fortune dropped in my lap now could give me half the thrill that that plain, modest little Estey organ did then...no grand piano was ever so sweet." Sallie explained the family's gradual migration to the growing town of Albany twenty-five miles away with a quote from Robert Lowell, "We need to be vitalized by contact with people." Since she had come to the Clear Fork of the Brazos, the buffalo had gone, the Indians had been settled on reservations, a fine ranch had been built, farmers had come, the homes had endured floods and the range had been ravaged by drought—the worst hitting in 1886.

When I visited Albany and saw the church the family had built

This soaring stackloader of silver-weathered wood on the Gang Ranch in British Columbia has been replaced by the hay baler.

Tackroom, Cartwright Ranches, Alberta

Without a variety of fuels, the modern ranch cannot exist.

Long replaced by the pick-up truck on most ranches, the chuckwagon still has the beauty of a truly functional object.

there, and read of their role in starting a school and a bank, and of Sallie's husband becoming a judge, I saw that the families at Lambshead had followed the classic settler's path, creating towns out of an eagerness to put behind them the hard side of frontier life the moment they could. Although other family members have stayed with or returned to ranching, Watt is the only one who now lives at Lambshead. Surrounded by the houses, he lives in a single room in the old bunkhouse. "I used to live in the big house. We'd have lots of company and I'd move down to the bunkhouse, and finally stayed."

In his eighty-four years, he has embraced much change. His cattle are worked by helicopter, a cheaper and faster way of cutting, sorting and driving cattle if you have a good aerial cowboy at the controls, he believes, than by horse. But, as a saddlemaker said, the methods may have changed but the man's the same. At Lambshead, the legacy of the past remains an integral part of daily ranching life, and as long as Watt Matthews is in charge, the ghosts will have a home. And the hospitality and sociability that characterized ranch life in an earlier era is maintained, perhaps to belie Watt's mother's concern. "We always seemed to have plenty of leisure time in those days. There never was any great hurry to be going. Now we have every convenience to make housekeeping easy and light...automobiles with paved roads to run them over...yet we have so little time for visiting...."

"We come here for the visiting as much as the rodeo," says Jerry Bracewell, making coffee at her camp in the pine forest campground at the Anahim Lake Stampede. "When you're ranching, you're tied to a cow's tail all year round." The hunger for contact and festivity that punctuated Sallie Reynold's pioneer life at Lambshead with get-togethers still exists in British Columbia's wild Chilcotin country, the most northerly outpost of the ranching culture that originated in Mexico. The legacy that must be carefully preserved in Texas still flares with full vitality at the campfires at Anahim Lake. Chilcotin, a vast wilderness that stretches from the Cariboo's borders at the Fraser River west to the Pacific coastal mountains, is regarded even by the rough-and-ready Cariboo as the last true wild west.

Considered the most authentic and exuberant of the western rodeos, the Anahim Lake Stampede is still close to rodeo's origin as a spontaneous event that used to be held on ranches to hone cowboys' skills and have some fun. You still sit on the corrals, in clouds of dust, with your boots dangling into the ring. White paper beer cups build up into snowdrifts over the three-day weekend. There are more Indian cowboys competing than whites. And the best all-round cowboy wins just a few hundred dollars, compared to the many thousands that ProRodeo's winners take away.

Above all, Anahim Lake Stampede is the cowboys' and ranchers' spiritual sanctuary. Forced to a marginal existence by the unstable economics of cattle and by the relaxed and sometimes inefficient traditional ranching style of the Cariboo-Chilcotin, the old ranching families were selling out, giving way, through the 1970s, to wealthy Europeans and others. Lumbering has replaced ranching as the top status occupation. The rancher feels fenced in by government controls that threaten to curb his independence. His herds are harassed by wolf and grizzly, predators he is no longer allowed to kill freely. And most of his rodeos have been coopted by tourists. The annual July stampede in Williams Lake, the Cariboo's major town, draws world-ranked cowboys and summer crowds, but the campfires that used to glitter on the hill at night are gone. But at Anahim, dozens of fires still glow in the campground, horses' tails swish in counterpoint to the rhythm of guitars, and talk and singing continue until sunup, when ranchers stumble to their sleeping bags for a few hours.

As her sons keep the fire fed, Jerry Bracewell reminisces about the great days: "We used to drive cattle twenty days from the Chilcotin to the annual cattle sale at Williams Lake. In those days, the rancher was king. There was no logging, no mining, no tourists, no resorts. Ranchers supported the town. They always put on a bash for us." As friends she hadn't seen for a year passed by, she pulled them into the fired ring and poured more coffee. "The ladies wore long gowns and gloves sent up from the coast by our relatives. I had taffeta and layers of net with big appliqued roses." Jerry talked about the wolf that "is putting us out of business. They've just killed twenty-six head of a rancher who can't afford to lose more than three or four." I listened to her tales of outpaddling a grizzly that was chasing her across an icy mountain lake, and of beginning labor with her first child while deep in the forest of the old Bracewell ranch, alone, of setting wolf traps in a blizzard. I was moved to see her that night at the dance, making an occasion of it. Alone in the blue-jeaned, cowboy-booted crowd, whooping and stomping in a the tribal frenzy, she wore an elegant long plaid skirt and, as she danced,

Above: Abandoned bunkhouse near White Springs, Montana.

Below: This old lazy susan table at the OH Ranch is made from two different-sized wagon wheels, and decorated around the edge with various ranch brands. Another old wagon wheel has been used as a chandelier.

Right: Old saddle hand-made by G.R. Roberts of Helena, Montana, a well-known saddle-maker who was also an early patron of the western painter Charles Russell. The basket stamp pattern on the leather, and carving on cantle are enjoying re-newed popularity today, as interest grows in the decorated saddles and gear used by the old-time buck-aroos. Each cattle region developed its own style evolving out of the early Spanish and Mexican sad-dles, with Texas and California styles dominating the ranges east and west, respectively, of the Rockies.

Detail of carved cantle on Roberts saddle.

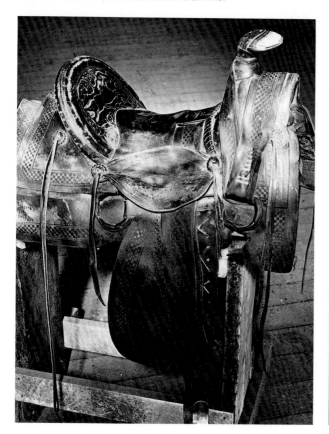

Bert Sheppard, one of the most famous of the old-time cowboys, who has seen the end of the open range and the Indian pony, reminisces at his OH ranch in Alberta.

163

neatly brushed ringlets bounced, belying thirty-five years as a rancher, trapper and big game guide.

Jerry sold her ranch a few years ago to a European industrialist and has moved to a log cabin at the edge of the wilderness to run her pack trips. It is remote, but it is her habitat. And, each summer, there is Anahim Lake. There, the rancher is still king.

In the old customs house on Monterey's docks, I fingered the folded cowhides, dried hard as iron, that are part of an even longer ranching legacy than Lambshead's. Cowhide like this had been the stuff of life during the rancho era that flourished on California's luxuriant coastal grasslands in the first half of the nineteenth century, the fullest flowering of the Spanish cattle culture in the New World. The cowhides had excited young Harvard student Richard Henry Dana, the author of *Two Years Before the Mast*, as he watched the ritual of loading the hides aboard the British and New England merchantmen that plied the California coast trading for hides and tallow, the ranchero's only products. Attending feasts and fandangos, experiencing the splendid and flamboyant style of dress and speech that distinguished even the humblest Californio, Dana had marveled that "a common bullock-driver, on horseback, delivering a message, seemed to speak like an ambassador at a royal audience."

The California rancheros, inheritors of the lands opened by the conquistador and mission padres who spread the Spanish presence from its base in central and South America, became, for a few brief decades, grandees in a unique frontier aristocracy. Merging Spanish grandeur with an intimate bond to the land, soldiers-turned-cattlemen developed a style of life in which amusements ranged from courtly fandangos to the bloody spectacle of grizzly bears and bulls battling to the death. Never walking if they could ride, the ranchero and his vaqueros may have been the world's best horsemen, with more silver than Dana had ever before seen glittering on their saddles, spurs and bridles.

The era is evoked, too, by a wedding dress of cream silk moiré with flounces of Valencia lace and sweeping train, kept under glass in the Santa Barbara Historical Museum. It had been worn by fourteen-year-old Dona Anita de la Guerra de Noriega y Corillo at her wedding at the Santa Barbara mission to Alfred Robinson, trading agent for the shipping company Dana sailed for, an event that had Dana on the deck of the ship unleashing a twenty-three-gun salute as the bride emerged from the church.

Anita had been the youngest daughter of "the grandee of the place, and the head of the first family in California." A titled Spaniard with a castle in Santander, and for many years commandant of the military presidio in Santa Barbara, José de la Guerra y Noriega had, in 1837, been granted grazing land on the peninsula at Point Conception, forty miles north of Santa Barbara, to raise cattle for the presidio. The de la Guerra holdings on these hills lush with filaree and burr clover, swelled over generations to a half-million-acre domain encompassing some of the most productive natural grassland in North America.

The old Rancho San Julian, de la Guerra's ranch headquarters, is one of the rare ranchos still held by blood heirs of the original Spanish grantee. Though San Julian has shrunk now to the home ranch, its grasslands are still unplowed, and the descendents of de la Guerra have held on. Seventy-six-year-old Dibblee Poett has devoted his life to maintaining his legacy. A courtly gentleman wearing a panama hat and white slacks as though for a Renoir picnic, he lifts his hat and ushers me past the white picket fence and into the garden of the rancho's old adobe—a home that grew, wing by wing, from a simple shelter for Spanish priests and soldiers travelling through to the U-shaped casa that became the ranch house for the burgeoning de la Guerra family. Today, the *casa* has a façade of white-painted wood sheathing the original adobe brick, and colonial-style white columns embellishing the deep Spanish corridors. As with Poett himself, a New England exterior has been laid over a strong Spanish base. Inside, the house is furnished with a melange of Spanish, Philippine, Chinese, English and New England furnishings gleaned from the trading ships that once filled Santa Barbara's harbor.

But, like the garden, the forces of change are beginning to get ahead of Poett. Strolling past rangy stalks of hollyhock, lavish eruptions of roses, ferns and daisies, and cascades of purple wisteria that flourish in this Mediterranean climate, Poett admits, "We can't afford to run the ranch, but we still do. We'd rather have the ranch than the money." He has had to sell off bits and pieces of the land over the years to pay inheritance and land taxes; the Jalama Ranch, at Conception Point, is now owned by the Bixby Ranch Company. Poett no longer runs any sheep or large herds of cattle; most of the grazing land is leased out to neighboring ranchers. His last cattle drives were along highways with highway patrolmen acting as outriders, their flashing red lights protecting his cows. The drives came to a crashing end when one of his bulls collided with a Greyhound bus, killing itself and seriously damaging the bus and injuring several passengers. As land values soar and Santa Barbara and Los Angeles expand, he searches for ways to hold San Julian as grazing land and make a living. He is mining and selling the ranch's diatomaceous earth. "We might augment our income by renting hunting privileges if we could introduce wild turkeys," he speculates.

Under a gnarled mission grapevine that, for a century, has spread mottled shade over the long arbor, Poett tells the stories that breathe life into his heritage. They are the stories spun each summer as he and his fellow members of the Society of Los Alamos, a men's club dominated by descendants of original rancheros, gather, sometimes here, to celebrate the ranchos. Slipping easily into the spirit as he barbecues a thick cut of beef, Poett sips Spanish sherry and sings snatches of the old Californio songs, lyrical, sentimental songs that he used to play on guitar. He chuckles as he recalls, "Forbes, a Yankee who came out on a whaler, came to a fiesta at San Julian. The vaqueros were all lassoing the bull with their reatas, so he took his harpoon and harpooned the bull!" Poett's sister, Frederica, cuts into the laughter with a reminder of a more subtle way outsiders found to insinuate themselves into rancho life: "They married the de la Guerra daughters."

Poett picks up the theme. "Yes, de la Guerra sold to Orena after the drought of the 1860s. That was the death blow, the capitulation of the ranchos. But Orena married one of the de la Guerra daughters and kept the land in the family. Then the original Dibblee, a New York lawyer, bought it and married de la Guerra's granddaughter." It was a marriage that brought to the de la Guerra domain the gringo industriousness and good business sense the rancheros lacked."

But their quality of living may have more than compensated for their lack of enterprise. Moving more deeply into the past, Poett shows me the back vegetable garden that fed the rancho: the family, servants, vaqueros and sheepmen. Old barns and shearing chutes still flank the garden. In luxuriant rows and hills, eggplants, peppers, corn, tomatoes, squash, peaches and apricots still grow. This abundance was the core of the legendary rancho hospitality that still flourishes in Poett, as does the gentility and ease that once softened the frontier roughness. He finds a young bird caught inside the wire netting protecting a fig tree and, talking to it gently in Spanish, delicately releases it.

An uncertain future hovers over the enchanted garden. Poett has gained some energetic young allies; several of the young

Cattle drive on the Irvine Ranch, California. From Point Conception to Orange County, wherever cattle ranching and development coexist on old rancho lands, cattle drives have become anachronisms; highway police, acting as outriders must try to prevent the collision of cows and traffic.

heirs have come back to the ranch. Jim and Maryanne Poett have started a small herd of Santa Gertrudis and Brangus cattle. But it is still a tenuous dream, for they cannot yet live off the land and must work at other jobs to survive. Maryanne, a journalist who married into the family several years ago, clearly sees the dilemma of San Julian and the few surviving ranchos as she raises her own child on the ranch. "San Julian is my child's legacy, but the land as foodland is everyone's birthright. I know it's sentimental, but the question is whether it's going to be held together in the family as a land grant, or whether it's more important to keep it agricultural even if it means selling it to cattlemen, or leasing it and not living here any more."

Lambshead and San Julian are preserved with more dedication than most ranches, but wherever I went in ranching country, in Texas or New Mexico, Wyoming, British Columbia or California, I found the legacy of the past was still strong. It might not always contribute to the efficiency of modern ranching, but it does reinforce the ranchers' pride and commitment, and gives their lives an enviable richness.

167

THE LIFE

Cattle drive on the Padlock
Ranch in Montana.

Julia-Lyn Davis, a lawyer in Santa Fe, still comes home often to the CS Ranch.

A member through birth and marriage of two of New Mexico's most distinguished ranching families, the Mitchells and Springers, Linda Davis heaves the hay that is vital to the wintering of the CS Ranch's 3,000-head cow herd at Cimarron. Summing up the challenges of ranching, she says, "To cope with all the elements and a year-round ranching operation, you have to be hardy and creative, and have a lot of the pioneering instinct."

Powder River rancher Bobby Gibbs's dislike for government interference matches his dislike for the predators who put him out of the sheep business. The Powder River region of Wyoming was one of the last and richest grassland areas to be opened to cattle in the late 1870s.

Branding is done the traditional way at Douglas Lake
Cattle Company, with cowboys cutting and roping the
calves from horseback, and throwing, holding and branding the calf by hand. In a few wildly active and noisy
minutes, the calf is branded, vaccinated, dehorned and has
its ears notched—a ritual that identifies the calf, protects
it from disease and determines whether it's destined for
herd or table.

Foreman checking heat of branding iron.

Mike Ferguson says of his nearly half-century of cowboying in British Columbia's Cariboo, "Your face and backside might get a little weathered, but actually it's a pretty healthy life."

For student veterinarians, the spring branding of Douglas Lake Cattle Company's 6,000 calves offers the invaluable hands-on experience medical students might get in the emergency ward of a large urban hospital. *Above:* A student veterinarian with a can of antiseptic spray at the ready. *Right:* Performed deftly by this cowboy girl, castration determines the future of a male calf as either a breeding sire or beefsteak.

A foreman at the Padlock
Ranch, Wyoming.

An Alberta cowboy, Udo Schneider, cuddles Australian sheep dog pups, a breed with an exceptional skill for working with cattle.

Rick Ortega, Ladder Ranch
cowboy, New Mexico.

Cowboy Warren Zimmerman, Alberta. The satisfactions and wisdom that come from a lifetime of working with animals and the land.

Overleaf: Honing a knife during a rest spell at a branding on the JA Ranch in the Palo Duro Canyon.

In clothes as functional as the corrugated siding behind him, Cedar Nolan, foreman of the F Cross Ranch in west Texas, is clearly no dude.

Cowboy boots for go, not show.

Ranching near the northern climatic limits of the cattle country, Frank Gattey has learned that "You can't ranch if you've got any quit in you." He shares with his wife, Kelva (*left*) the work of running the Simmenthal herd at the Cross Bar Ranch, Consort, Alberta, where he was born.

Cowboys come in all sizes.

Fishermen's waders. Recreation is an important part of ranch economy.

Overleaf: At the end of a long day of branding at the Douglas Lake Cattle Company.

He may not have grown
up to his horse or belt
buckle yet, but he's already
riding with the cowboys.

A young cowboy watching
a rodeo.

Ken Smith, retired cowboy. Now over eighty, he has ridden five times from Canada to Mexico on cattle drives. As a boy, he learned many of his skills from the old-time vaqueros, including plaiting and braiding horsehair. Here, he holds some of the bridles and guitar bands he has made.

The horsehair is spun
before it is plaited.

Ranching, alone, out of the historic ghost town of Shakespeare in southern New Mexico, Rita Hill and her daughter Janaloo fight creosote bush, cactus and drought to graze their eighty-seven-head herd of cattle. They augment their income by running a ballet school in the ghost town for girls from nearby Lordsburg.

A grim day's work by the predator control helps to
protect Colorado sheep ranchers, near Meeker, from
coyotes which can devastate a crop of new lambs.

Bill Sallee, former cowboy and now mechanic on the
Ladder Ranch in southwest New Mexico, sells the handsome coyote pelts for $50 each.

Above: On the McIntyre Ranch's wildlife preserve in southern Alberta, the coyote can be seen, alert and handsome, as part of the natural symbiosis of the range. But rampant predation by wolf, bear, mountain lion, eagle and, above all, coyote, is one of the most serious threats stalking today's rancher. In a climate of emotion, rancher, hunters, environmentalists and government departments of fish and game try to find balances that will protect both wildlife and rancher.

Cupping his hands to his mouth, Bill Austin's call lures the coyotes within range of his rifle. Hunting by foot, truck and airplane, Austin, who is the coyote hunter for Johnson County, Wyoming, kills about 200 coyotes a year.

The Bolak Ranch in Farmington, New Mexico, is a wildlife exhibit and sanctuary as well as working cattle ranch.
Sixty thousand waterfowl, mainly Canada geese, are
fed up to three tons of corn cobs a day during winter.

In the trophy room, animals from around the world are
displayed.

Jimmy Nolan, snakehunter, on the F Cross Ranch at the southern end of the Texas Panhandle. When ranch owner Floyce Masterson Bates came to the ranch as a tenderfoot years ago and found a den of rattlers in her cellar, she had it boarded up, preserves and all.

Cowboy at Douglas Lake Cattle Company.

The mecca for lovers of good ropes is King Ropes in
Sheridan, Wyoming.

King also makes, repairs and sells commercial saddles. A
good saddle still costs a cowboy two month's wages, and a
custom hand-built one will cost him up to $3,000.

Having survived their first winter, these calves are less vulnerable to snow and cold weather than newborns. But blizzards can still kill cows, suffocating them under snowdrifts or making it impossible for the rancher to reach them with water and food.

Left: Every year, ranchers know they will lose a small percentage of their calf crop to calving problems, predators, disease or climate. Ranchers breed their cows so that calves will arrive after the heavy snows, knowing, as does Alberta rancher Catherine Gardner after fifty years of ranching, "It's better to be a late calf than a frozen-to-death one."

Watching birth, and then the process of licking, licking, licking a newborn, sometimes for hours, until it stumbles up from the snow for its first milk, Doolittle Ranch manager Cliff Copeland says, with a sense of awe, "No one teaches them how to do it. It's instinct. Whenever I see this, I feel so rich."

The historic Texas longhorn gallops back from the brink
of extinction to renewed popularity.

Artist and rancher Terry
Kelsey raises prize-winning
longhorns and celebrates
the dramatic revival of the
breed in dynamic bronze
sculptures. *Top right:*
Kelsey working on a wax
model that will be cast in
bronze.

Right: The Kelsey living
room near Kiowa,
Colorado.

Cowboy at Douglas County
Rodeo, at Castle Rock,
Colorado, waits his turn to
rope.

Silver snuffbox lid indicates importance of snuff, which, like chewing tobacco, has the advantages of freeing the hands, and not being a fire hazard. But rolling your own with one hand is still the mark of a true old-timer.

Cowboy at Evans Camp Ranch near Buford, Colorado, cold-shoeing his horse. A good all-round cowboy still takes pride in keeping the three or four horses he rides well shod.

Catherine Gardner brings such dignity even to well-worn riding gear that a neighbor said admiringly, "I'll bet she wears her pearls on a roundup." Of the Alberta ranch life she has shared for more than fifty years with her husband, Percy, at their Bluebird Valley Ranch, she says, "The young people care more about the politics and economics; we cared more about the life."

Allie Streeter, rancher, Nanton, Alberta. Any Canadian rancher seeing Allie Streeter's belt buckle knows that this CS brand means the Calgary Stampede, which honored Streeter for his pioneering work with the world-famous event. The first Stampede in 1912 was supposed to be a nostalgic look at a fast-vanishing west but the cattle culture is still alive and kicking, thanks to the commitment of ranchers such as Streeter.

Allie Streeter carrying his
favourite saddle.

It takes sweat and muscle to brand the traditional way, but cowboss Mike Ferguson at the Douglas Lake Cattle Company believes it's still faster and more efficient than the more modern branding chute or table.

Douglas Lake cowboys drive cows toward their calves for
"mothering-up" after branding.

Nicola Valley cowboys wait while calves and cows
"mother-up" after branding.

Class shows in how a cowboy rides, how he acts, and how
he looks. These are the chaps of a cowboy from the
Nicola Valley's Douglas Lake Cattle Company, one of the
diminishing number of ranches where it is possible to do
only cowboy's work.

Sheep shearers on the Crazy Woman Ranch in Buffalo, Wyoming—a region that is still a bastion both of sheep and of the Basque sheepmen who have brought their traditions and skills to the western ranges for more than a century. Here, the sheep are being "eyebrowed," literally getting the wool out of their eyes. At the same time, they are branded, though with paint, not a smoking iron.

Fencing, one of the most important and inescapable
of ranching chores.

THE LIFE

IT WAS 6 A.M. and still pitch black, but John Baucus had finished breakfast with the herders in the cookhouse and was getting the day's work set for the men who watched the grazing bands of black-faced ewes and cared for the young rams and sick sheep kept in pens here at the Sieben ranch, twenty-odd miles out of Helena, Montana. Lambing would start soon. By late March, the pace of lambing would reach 150 lambs every twenty-four hours, with a hand patrolling the length of the huge lambing shed all night, walking a scaffold built above the tiny "jugs," or pens, where the ewes and lambs are "forced to get acquainted," as John says, for the mothering instinct has faded in the highly-bred Rambouillet sheep. But the ranch was quiet now. He headed back to the house, where his three children were already pouring syrup on their french toast.

The house had been a roadside inn during the 1890s, where, for a dollar a night, two men could get a bed, meals and hay for their horses. It still looks the part, with its log exterior, a wide front porch and silvered antlers over the door. It has been in John Baucus's family since his great-grandfather, Henry Sieben, bought the ranch in 1896. It sits at the junction of the old freighting road from Helena north to Fort Benton and the military and cattle trail that once ran beyond Fort Benton and Walla Walla in the Washington Territory. Still standing beyond the house and the cookhouse is one of the cabins built by fur trader Malcolm Clark 120 years ago. Clark's grave is here too. He was shot by Peigan Indians while in the middle of a backgammon game with his daughter. Nina, John Baucus's wife, picks up arrowheads all the time in the garden and chicken yard.

Nina had known what she would be in for from her first date with John. "I helped him clean manure out of the sheds with the 'cat.' When the foreman saw me changing the cat blade, he asked John, 'When are you going to marry her?' You have to love it, because the economics aren't there. People aren't eating lamb or wearing wool. And how often would *you* work an eighteen-hour day?" Nina laughs. "I start at 5 a.m. during lambing, and I'm lucky to get to bed at midnight. Lambs are born at night, and you have to do a 10 p.m. and a 2 a.m. check, and be back out there at five." In some ways, though, sheep are easier than cattle. "Cattle couldn't *climb* some of this steep range. Sheep do better on forbs and shrubs than cows. They eat wild rose, aspen leaves and *any* weed." Nina adds, "And you don't have to fatten sheep in a feedlot—they can go straight from the range to slaughter."

Sheep have as long a history on the frontier as cattle. In California, many of the great cattlemen—Irvine, Bixby, Hollister—drove herds of sheep across the plains and the Sierra, and built their wealth and reputations as sheepmen. But economics gave cattle the ascendancy in numbers and status. "There used to be twenty-seven million sheep in Montana. Now there are less than a million," says John. "I think, in people's minds, cattle are so romantic." The Baucuses have cattle, too. "But we stay in sheep for the tradition. We're the fifth generation on this land."

While John goes into Helena to shop today, Nina will feed and collect eggs from her chickens, ducks and geese—"my menagerie!" She will supervise when the vet comes to treat cancer eye in some of the cows and catch up on her spinning. "There's more here for me than in Helena," she says, as she pulls carded wool from one of the paper bags of variegated gray Rambouillet wool that sit on the floor of the den—wool she washes in the kitchen sink, spins in the dryer, then spreads all over the floor to dry. Light pours through a large, lead-paned window onto a jungle of philodendron, cactus and rubber plants. Nina, in sweater and jeans, sits on a green, satin-striped sofa surrounded by fleeces and fat balls of slubbed wool, with the light warming the wood of her spinning wheel. John's oak rolltop desk, spread now with papers and a calculator, may soon hold an Apple II computer, a tool many younger ranchers believe may become as vital to ranching as John's $50,000 New Holland hay baler. "But we haven't been able to buy software yet that will work for sheep ranching," Nina says.

In Helena, John does his rounds, shopping for the herders:

Western Warehouse for canned goods, Union Market for meat, DeVore's Saddlery for gear and work clothes. When shearing is finished in June, the herders will trail the sheep on a three-day drive to the wide ranges of the Continental Divide, just over the snow-topped mountains to the west, and set up summer camp. The bright blue camp, shaped like a covered wagon but roofed with corrugated steel, with horses tethered close by, could be a Gypsy caravan. With a chimney cut through the roof, the herder's litttle wagon is bunkhouse and cookhouse for weeks at a time. A foreman visits the herders once a week, taking them food and telling them when to move camp. Sheep can go longer than cattle without water, but, moving in bands of 1,200, they easily overgraze the grass. "And you have to keep an eye on the herders. Some are a little afraid, and they bunch the sheep up all together so that they can't graze. They're hungry at the end of the day, and on a moonlit night they get up and *leave*," says John. "They scatter and split into smaller and smaller bunches, and then a coyote picks them off." Herders always carry a coyote gun. "They used to be all Basques. Now they're more Peruvians," says Nina. "And it's not a fiction that some of them are rich men from the east who want to escape from society. They're loners."

In the old frame house on the Padlock Ranch's Ash Creek camp that's home to cowboy Jack Cooper, Jack picks up his guitar and starts to strum and sing. His wife, Dorothy, sitting on the sofa, leans slightly toward him with a look that even after ten children and thirty-four years of marriage could only be called adoration. Jack tells me, "We built the first house we ever lived in. Dorothy and me cut the trees ourself, skidded them down with a team, hewed 'em by hand. It cost us $179. We'd like to build our last one.

"A good cowboy always has a job. We raised ten kids by punching cows, and we never went hungry," Jack says. "There were things we went without, but we never bought anything we couldn't pay cash for. A lot of these old cowboys, they may not have much. But they're going to die without debt. They'd lay down their life for a friend, but they don't want to owe anybody." Jack earns $600 a month, plus house and utilities. For Jack, his wealth lies not in the wages, but in the life he's lived, a life so appealing that three of his boys have become cowboys. "When I was just a kid in the big drought in the '30s, I trailed my daddy's cattle all over western South Dakota trying to find grass. One time, I had a quarter in the spring, and that fall I had that same quarter, shiny as you can imagine, and I'd had room and board,

Hungry cattle waiting for round bales of hay to be unrolled for their daily dinner. Mechanization like this on the DD Ranch in Ridgeway, Colorado, has speeded and eased the arduous job of winter hay handling.

Pumped by windmills in much of the ranch country, water holes must be kept open through ice-locked winters on the high plains east of Denver.

Round-up on the rolling grasslands of the Douglas Lake
Cattle Company in British Columbia.

Helicopter round-up,
Lambshead Ranch, Texas.

and so much fun! They were hard times, but you had so many friends. They'd let you take your cattle across their property, and share their water."

It was the big Wyoming ranges that originally attracted Jack. "That's what brought us from South Dakota twenty-seven years ago," says Dorothy. "He wanted to get on a bigger outfit where he didn't have to do anything but ride." "The very root of the whole thing is freedom," he says. "I think pride's the basis of it," Dorothy adds. Padlock once tried to promote him for foreman, but he preferred it back on the Ash Creek camp where he could just be a cowboy. With most of the kids gone, Dorothy rides with him now. "She rides like a wild Indian," he hoots. "She does a thirty-five mile circle. Circle is the cowboys' name for a day's work. It might be square, it might be oblong, you might go straight out and straight in. But we call it a circle. She gets a kick out of watching some old coyote trailing after us," he says fondly. "That's where you see how much they love what they do," says Dorothy, looking too young, small and fragile to be a hard-riding mother of ten.

With the good-natured reticence that characterizes many cowboys, Jack admits, "Roping bulls can get pretty thrilling. On the bull roundup in the fall, some of those old bulls are mad. We leave about 120 of them out for about sixty days—one bull for every twenty cows—and they kind of go back to their old wild nature and don't want to come in. But I take two dogs and a six-shooter full of birdshot to get them out of that old brush, and that gets their attention." Then he chuckles at a memory. "Riding a bucking horse isn't bad. There's no metal or flying parts when you have a wreck. But you can get killed with a rope as easy as anything, you bet. One thing cowboys love to do is rope—anything!" And he's off on a hilarious account of a cowboy on a bucking horse roping a tree'd bear.

For Jack Cooper, Padlock is one of the best and biggest outfits in Wyoming. "But I might get the urge to get on a bigger place yet," Jack says. "The more room I've got, the more cattle I can move. My son breaks horses for the ZX in Paisley, Oregon. They've got 1,300,000 acres! This is better grass country. But they run 30,000 head of cattle. And their cowboy crew does no fencing, no farming, no haying. All they do is punch cows. In Nevada and Oregon, there are a lot of places like that any more," he says, using the vernacular of the region. "There's still a big cattle country that people don't know anything about." Dorothy has seen this sparkle in his eyes before. "My son and me had just moved 1,300 head of cattle straight up and straight down in the roughest country you can find. My son called from Paisley and said, 'Five of us just moved *6,000* head!' I get awful restless. I read about those big outfits in Nevada. I've always wanted to work in the desert. There's a place in Nevada that's 120 miles from town. That's where I'd like to go. Dorothy, can go to town one year, and I'll go the next," he says, letting out a bellow of laughter that could be heard over four sections.

A cowboy, his hat, head and shoulders bobbing above the grease-wood, rolls through the range looking for strays near the long road back to Ladder Ranch headquarters, land so tough that it takes leased government lands as well as the ranch's own 600 sections to graze 2,500 head of mother cows. The scene is classic. But home on the range—on the Ladder Ranch, at least—has changed.

An empty jeroboam of Pontet Latour '75, signed by guests of the owner Robert O. Anderson, decorates the lounge of the hunting lodge furnished with the tan leather chairs where ceiling fans move the air in the summer heat of this southern New Mexico range. The room hosts corporate presidents, movie stars and ambassadors, who fly in to hunt and ride with Anderson, whose twelve ranches in Texas and New Mexico make him the largest landowner in the U.S. "When I was cowboying here before, that used to be the bunkhouse," says Bill Sallee, pointing his hammer at the handsome two-story stone building. "The cowboys used to sit out on that long screened porch in the evening, work on their saddles and gear, and drink a lot of beer." Bill is now a mechanic, repairing the fourteen pickups and several dozen pump jacks and motors for the wells and windmills that keep the Ladder Ranch running. Bill is hammering at the drive train underneath the Ford pickup up on the hoist. "I worked as a cowboy all over—here, Colorado, Montana, Wyoming, Arizona. I rodeoed—bull riding, saddle bronc, bareback. But my wife decided I should retire when my last eighteen horses fell with me," he says. "I worked in Los Angeles as a greaser mechanic, but when they made me production manager, I came back to where the pace is a little slower."

There is a certain irony in the bumper sticker on the truck he's repairing: "Used Cowboy, Very Cheap." Reentering cowboy life is not easy. The trucks and equipment he services have reduced the number of cowboys the vast ranch used to keep. In the compound by the old bunkhouse where Bill works, the sun is strong, and a cowboy in boots, spurs and beaten-up black cowboy hat leans against a GMC pickup, visiting with the welder mending a metal branding chute, sending sparks flying.

It isn't just mechanization that's changed ranching. The number of wealthy owners who are lured to ranching for its tax incentives and prestige, as well as for the land and cattle, is growing as ranch economics force many old-time ranchers to sell to men with the corporate sophistication and capital to weather the vicissitudes of the cattle industry. But many of these men, Robert Anderson among them, have a profound commitment to ranching and are deeply involved in the work.

Joe Gardner, who manages Canada's largest privately owned ranch, the Douglas Lake Cattle Company, covers the continent as casually as cowboys used to cover the range. "I'll be in Alberta on Saturday, Sunday in Chicago, and then San Antonio for the International Stockman's Foundation conference," he says. "I'll check the horses in Texas, and then fly through San Francisco on the way home." The ranch's owner since, 1959, "Chunky" Woodward, developed a cutting horse operation, and keeps his world champion, Peppy San, at stud in Gainesville, Texas, where the stallion commands breeding fees as high as $20,000. "The foals generated in Texas supply the ranch too, so we've got trailers going back and forth between Douglas Lake and Texas," says Joe. He and his cowboss, Mike Ferguson, no longer go to Alberta and Montana as often to buy the fifty replacement bulls they need each year, but they travel to sales around B.C. The sense of lively involvement in the larger ranching world is emphasized by the roar of the Citation II Woodward flies in to the asphalt strip by the front door of his house at the home ranch several times a month, and by the daily coming and going of the ranch's workhorse Cessna 185 and the small planes of visitors coming to experience what the former manager's wife, Nina Woolliams, called "the ranch's glamorous simplicity."

Douglas Lake's setting in a somewhat remote valley has allowed it—like the great King Ranch in Texas—to evolve a society as self-contained as that of a feudal manor. Even today, as you turn off the highway onto the road to Douglas Lake, you begin to feel a cozy insularity. Firewood cut from the Ponderosa pine forest is neatly stacked in small pyramids by the side of the road. Hay bales, square, round and loaf-shaped, are stored for use. High golden bunch grass and grain carpet the valley floor and gentle foothills that lead past the old ranches that have shared the history of Nicola Valley—the Guichon, Stump Lake, Quilchena—to tiny Douglas Lake, site of the home ranch. One of the four ranches into which the sprawling half million acres is divided, and known as English Bridge, it is an orderly and attractive compound of white painted frame buildings and corrals by the water's edge. It is a place of structure. In addition to the four subranches, there are ten cow camps, four hay ranches, eight leased grazing units and so many fences that, as a cowboy said, "they give you claustrophobia!" "We're almost self-sufficient," says Joe. "If a doom and gloom situation came, this ranch could get by without outside help."

The store is also the post office and social center for the ranch. Indians from the neighboring Quilchena reservation drive over in their pickups to shop and visit. Few of them work on the ranch, but since the first British hunting party came through the valley in 1863 and found them living by the Nicola River, they have been part of the culture, one with a certain patriarchal style. An elderly woman with most of her teeth missing is helped into the ranch office by a younger woman. She has come to do her banking, and is greeted and joked with, for, a close relative of a former cowboss, Joe Coultee, she is part of the family. A portrait of Coultee, whose colorful reputation was enhanced by his having branded his woman one day, hangs on the office wall. Although the ranch has lost its connection to the founding family, the owners, managers and cowbosses have had remarkably long tenures. Joe Gardner is only the fifth manager in well over a century. Mike has been cowboss for thirty-two years—half his life. Chunky Woodward, the "new" owner, has had the ranch for a quarter of a century. The Ward family stayed involved from 1884 to 1950. And the style for the first several generations was strongly British, as it was on most of western Canada's early ranches. The first known white men in the valley were the members of a hunting party organized by Clement Cornwall, the pioneer rancher who settled on land just to the north. Cornwall and others like him sought to transplant English country life to the frontier, interspersing their ranching activities with shooting, polo, tennis and formal meals served from silver platters by white-uniformed Indian girls.

"Sunday is just another day to a cow," says Douglas Lake cowboss Mike Ferguson as he drives the mile-long corridor where thousands of his young cattle munch hay along the fence line. Mike's preoccupation is ensuring that his cattle destined for

Having started as a
cowboy, Joe Mimms now
manages a ranching
empire that covers large
areas of Texas and New
Mexico, including the
Ladder Ranch, with a head
office here at Roswell,
New Mexico. Although
he spends a lot of time
on the phone and in an
airplane, he says "You
must be willing to go out
and get dirty with the
guys."

Curry Holden, water witcher.

Above: Gordon Cartwright saddling up one of the Arabian horses he breeds for ranch work on his D Ranch in the Alberta foothills. Many cattlemen prefer the quarter horse, which combines the explosively fast and sensitive movement of the Arabian with the thoroughbred's acceleration and cow sense.

The human urge to put one's own brand on an impersonal mobile home expresses itself in the lavish stand of hollyhocks, the attached shed hung with artifacts of the range, and the welcoming strip of artificial grass laid down over concrete.

233

the Panorama sale, to be held on the ranch in September, reach the sale at optimum health, weight and finish. The prices per pound he will get there will not only set the operating budget for the next year, but be a measure of the reputation of his Hereford herd. Ranchers are extremely loyal to the breeds of their choice. Mike sticks to his faith in Herefords in an era when more and more ranchers are playing musical genes, cross-breeding such standard breeds as Hereford and Angus with half a dozen "exotic" breeds to get faster-gaining, beefier cattle. "We've started a small crossbreeding program," says Mike, "but we'll keep the main herd Hereford. I think there will always be a place for Hereford."

In the steamy languor and mesquite-whiskered range of the south Texas coast, breeding programs have been as much a response to the climate as to the market. The King Ranch has systematically evolved both cattle and quarterhorses custom-tailored to its unique conditions. In a climate that's hard on both people and animals, it has evolved the Santa Gertrudis, the only uniquely American breed, a beefy rust-red cross of shorthorn and Brahman.

Few breeds have developed as enthusiastic a following as the Texas longhorn recently has. Darol Dickinson of Calhan, Colorado, is in Denver to join longhorn breeders from a dozen states who have come to the Denver National Western Stock Show to show and sell their cattle and to celebrate the breed. This is the first year that the "Super Bowl of stock shows" has dignified the longhorn by judging it along with all the other "respectable" breeds.

Moving on from a career as a successful western artist, Dickinson is reviving this previously castoff breed, employing genetic engineering and aggressive selective breeding. Just thirteen years ago, the Texas longhorns that had virtually fathered the cattle industry were closer to extinction than the buffalo, preserved as a kind of living national monument in two government refuges and in a small state herd in Texas. A rangy nomad with horns grotesquely wide in proportion to its scrawny frame, the longhorn had been abandoned by a growth-obsessed industry in favor of the long-framed, beefy breeds. But as a result of its wanderings on the most terrible of southwestern wastelands, the longhorn had developed certain traits Darol Dickinson felt all cattlemen wanted: small calves, born unassisted on the range, but gaining weight fast after birth—for gainability is essential;

and browsing skills, for the longhorn had learned to fatten up on range where most other breeds would starve. They were fertile animals, maturing young enough that you could usually get an extra calf out of a cow in her lifetime, and long lived, producing a calf a year for up to 30 years back in the mesquite.

But, scrutinizing the animal with an artist's eye, Dickinson knew it wouldn't do. If you could just make it look a little more like a Hereford—straighten the back a bit, and fill out the scrawny hollows in the flanks and shoulders.... With an almost biblical disregard for the time constraints of evolution, he set about to shape up the longhorn. "In just 13 years, he went from $300 longhorns the banks wouldn't even lend money on to selling a twenty-four-month-old bull, Impressive, for $60,000," says Patty Jones, the account executive for the active advertising and promotional side of the business. By 1982, Texas longhorn numbers had grown to 40,000 and bulls were becoming popular as sires for a heifer's first calf for the breeds that had calving problems. Showing color photographs of the longhorn before, and since, Dickinson, Patty says, "took a scraggly animal that wasn't much to look at and, today, has beef conformation that beef cattlemen want, but enough color and horn length that purebred herds want too." The dramatic elongation of the great curving sweeps of horn are, she says, "just tradition. They don't really *do* anything." How could such transformation take place so fast? Darol had bought or borrowed bulls and cows that had the traits he wanted to intensify, and shifted the speed of selective breeding into the space age. No more haphazard following of sexual instinct here. To spread the genes of the best animals as far, and as fast, as he could, Darol collected, used and sold semen for artificial insemination, and flushed fertilized eggs out of 50 prize purebred cows, implanting the embryos in other cows so that the best cows' egg production would not be slowed by having to carry the calves themselves. "We superovulate the donor cows so that we get an average of eighteen eggs per year per cow. The donor cows do kind of burn out after five or six years, but we get maybe 100 calves from them during their lifetimes."

Driven to black humor by the explosion of super-breeding, an old rancher, reading literature at an embryo transplant booth at the Denver stock show, shook his head and said, "Hitler would have been right at home here." But, then, so would Betty Grable. "Darol's just insured Sweet 'N Low's horns for half a million dollars," said Patty, "She's the longest horned heifer yet."

Matt Eberle pulled out the saddle pieces, eager to show me how Norm Stearns's saddle was going to look. His little saddlemaking shop in High River, Alberta, draws some of the biggest cattlemen and rodeo stars in the business. But 85 percent of his customers are cowboys. "It's funny," Matt says, "it always took two months' wages to buy a plain saddle, no matter what wages were. If a top cowboy gets $700 now, his basic saddle is still going to cost him $1,600." This would not be a basic saddle. He'd never met Norm Stearns before he walked into the shop just a few months before. "But I knew him by name. When I was cowboying over in the Nicola Valley in B.C. at Douglas Lake and Guichon, he'd been there before me. A good cowboy always leaves a name." Norm had worked the good outfits; a 1965 article on the big McIntyre Ranch on the Alberta-Montana border showed a picture of a square-jawed Norman Stearns, in cowboy hat and denim jacket, cinching up a plain, working saddle.

"Norm walked in here one day and said, 'You going to build me a saddle? I want to spend about $3,000. What can you do for me?'" Matt pulled out pieces of tan cowhide, already cut and richly carved into skirts and fenders, and laid them on the tree, or frame, showing me how a saddle was built up, layer upon layer. Skirts, fenders, cantle, fork, seat, horn, stirrups. "Norm had figured out a saddle through the years. He wanted it full carved, with six silver conches. It's more a modernized buckaroo style, with a very slick fork, a large horn and a very deep seat like the old Visalia saddle that stems off the Mexican style—the kind of saddle that goes with the spade-bit guys like Norm. The really finessy cowboys with a hair-trigger rein."

Norm wanted it California carved, with ripple-petaled copper roses worked into a continuous twining of leaves and tendrils, the elaborate carving of the Visalia saddle tradition. Most of the carving would be done at night, or early in the morning. Once you got the cowhide "cased-up," or wet through, you had to work it all at once, when it was quiet and you could pour yourself into it, undisturbed. "You've got to have a nice feeling for it if you're cutting a curved line. Your fingers have to be as sensitive as a safecracker's—it's the same as poetry." Hundreds of metal carving tools are stacked in pockets on a shelf within easy reach of the polished granite slab Matt uses as his carving bench. "Cliff Ketchum, the man who taught me, said, 'If you love a lady, you don't go about her crudely.' It's finesse, you know." Rubbing fingers over the high-carved copper rose, Matt exhibited a sensuousness that seldom shows through a cowboy's

At the granite work table in his saddlery in High River, Alberta, Matt Eberle works on cowboy Norm Stearn's $3000 saddle. When it comes to carving the roses and vines into wet leather, this saddle-maker says, "You've got to have fingers as sensitive as a safecracker's. It's the same as poetry."

few words and plain talk. "Cowboys are the softest guys you ever saw. They're the most religious people in their own way. Have you ever been close to death? Once you've been banged up on a horse a couple of times, that's when you really see how nice the trees grow. Your friends look a lot better to you. A lot of people go through life without the highs and lows a cowboy knows; they never hit the high plateaus. The toughest old cowboys appreciate the sky, the green grass, the flowers."

When he's done about eighty hours of carving on Norm's saddle, he'll attach the silver. It's nickel silver, harder than sterling, engraved and made up by a silversmith in High River the way Norm wants it. There'll be a silver horn cap, Norm's initials on the back of the Cheyenne roll, the oval conches on the front and rear seat jockeys and back housing where the rawhide strings come through. There'll be a small set of saddle bags, a small staple pouch for patching fences and a fencing plier case. "He'll be using this saddle when he starts riding this spring. He's riding now for a lease outfit near Brooks, about sixty miles east. In Nevada, where it's sandy and dry, you only get eight or ten years from a saddle, but in Alberta they last a lot longer.

"Norm's 67 now. He figures he has another 20 years of riding," Matt chuckles, his eyes twinkling with affection for cowhide "that's tough and soft at the same time," and for old cowboys. "This'll be the first saddle he's ever really had made the way he would like it made. It'll be his last saddle, eh?"

POSTSCRIPT

When I came to North America from England thirty years ago, I naturally first encountered the eastern seaboard. Though it is very different from Britain, there is nevertheless in the east a pastoral and landscaped quality to the scenery that had some similarity to the British countryside. But many years later, when traveling in the west, taking photographs for my book *Summer Places*, I became fascinated and almost overwhelmed by the vast scale of these lands which did not have the patina of constant human use. I was tremendously drawn to ranches and to the ranch life that gave me a human contact with this magnificent country. Inevitably I was reminded of the first cowboy films I had seen as a youth, and was delighted to find arid and sculptured scenery that looked as though it had been the location for those old western films. I became determined to explore these romantic and splendid rangelands.

Photography has always been for me a process of exploration and discovery, and an opportunity to respond to things which interest and move me. Since it was the landscape of the west that had originally attracted me, this was what I first began to photograph, trying to come to terms with problems of distance and spatial relationships. But also increasingly fascinating were the buildings and artifacts that are associated with ranching life. And as I traveled through the west, it was the people who live there, who offered me so freely their time, hospitality and friendship, that made the final impression.

Almost by chance, the first ranch I visited was the wonderfully preserved Lambshead ranch in Texas. The character of its buildings and landscape, its history, camaraderie and atmosphere combine in a way that has come to represent ranching for me. I visited a great many other ranches and came to appreciate their tremendous variety, from the enormous ones such as the Douglas Lake Cattle Company and the Padlock Ranch that are almost overpowering in their immensity, to the Buckley family ranch where I saw how this magnificent land could be ranched on a much smaller scale. Here, in a small beautiful canyon off the Powder River in Wyoming, a man, his wife and their two young sons ranch entirely on their own. They live their remote life because they just want to be there more than anywhere else in the world. This is not just a romantic notion, it is very real, and also in a sense, quite typical. Nearly all ranchers have the conviction that their own land is very special and unique, and, on the other hand, many of them share the feeling that they are not ultimately owners of their land, but rather custodians or stewards.

In the harsh economic times of today, hundreds of ranches are being foreclosed, and many of the ways of the Old West are gone forever. But as long as the grazing of cattle is an efficient way of converting grass to protein, certain of the ways of ranching will survive, and so will the satisfaction and romance of enduring a life which combines the vagaries of land, animals, weather and man. These challenges, too, are enduring.

Dudley Witney

ACKNOWLEDGMENTS

Hundreds of people in the ranching world from British Columbia to Texas gave of their time, help and hospitality as we were preparing this book. Their generosity and friendship have provided us with an incomparable experience. We both feel a special appreciation for the sensitivity and encouragement Miriam Shelton Deane has brought to the project. We would like to thank the following:

Joe Alexander
Dale and Betty Alsager
Robert Anderson
Robert Armstrong
William and Floyce Bates
Sonni Bone
Richard Bonnycastle
Max W. Bradshaw
John Brittingham
Dean Brookie
William and Mollie Canaday
Gordon Cartwright
John Cartwright
Jim Cerruti
George Chattaway
Phillip and Betty Clark
Dee Cole
Alvin G. Davis
Les and Linda Davis
Peter and Deedee Decker
William J. Dickerson
Barbara Doolittle
Peter and Philae Dominick
Robert Edgar
George Ewing
Flemming Fischer
Chuck Forsman
Joe and Sam Gardner
Frank and Kelva Gattey
Bobby and Martha Gibbs
Royce and JoAnn Griggs
Bert Hargraves
Dr. Harold Heady
Curry and Frances Holden
Dave Holden
Leslie Holden
Robert and Arlene Hohnstock
The Irvine Ranch
Dr. Alex Johnston
Sallie Judd
Melville Kendrick

Joan Kerr
Neltze Kings
David and Kendy La Chapelle
Kristin Lewis
David MacKenzie
Sid and Myrna Marty
Watt Matthews
Larry McKay
John Meigs
Thomas Merlan
Perry Minor
Simon and Dollie Oberlin
Gordon Parke
Linda Parke
William and Stella Pence
Dibblee Poett
Frederica Poett
Dorothy Prior
Dean Prosser
Richard Reese
Monte Ritchie
Pat and Irene Rutledge
Dan S. Scott
Dave Scott
Hal and Mary Shelton
Peter and Ellen Shelton
Bert Sheppard
Sheilagh Simpson
Dr. Syd B. Slen
Ken Smith
Stan Steiner
Mons L. Teigen
Oakleigh and Lisa Thorne
Arthur Townsend
Sandra Treuenfels
Bob Turnell
John Vandiver
Pamela Witney
Dr. Theodore Wood
Charles Woodward
Henriette Wyeth